HONG KONG

LOCAL

HONG KO

CULT RECIPES FROM THE STRE

NG LOCAL

ARCHAN CHAN

PHOTOGRAPHY BY ALANA DIMOU

S THAT MAKE THE CITY

Smith
Street
Books

EARLY
8

MID
66

LATE
104

BASICS
166

Introduction

In just a few hundred years, Hong Kong has gone from a small farming and fishing community to an international free port and global financial centre. It is regularly the most visited city in the world – with more than 25 million people travelling to the city every year.

Food is an integral part of any country's or city's culture, history and lifestyle and Hong Kong is no exception. Hong Kong's cuisine has been characterised as a fusion of East and West, reflecting the cultural diversity and the influence of its Chinese roots, the years of British Colony and the current day cosmopolitan 'world city'.

As an international metropolitan hub, Hong Kong brings together different cuisines from all over the world. Elevated by its incredibly diverse local food, Hong Kong has been praised as a food paradise for decades.

curry fish balls

You'll find something incredible to eat in Hong Kong at any time of the day, and there is something for every type of diner – from humble, traditional breakfasts like congee; or quick and satisfying noodles for lunch from one of the many small local shops; to trendy streetside treats like bubble tea and egg waffles, and feasts of roast meats and the highest of high-end Michelin-starred dining experiences the world has to offer.

EA

RLY

Early

Wandering the streets of Hong Kong at 6 am is quite an experience. The sky starts to lighten over the harbour, heralding the beginning of another new day for a city that never seems to sleep.

In the early morning, most of the shops stay closed while the cooks in congee stores, soy product shops, *cha chaan teng* (Hong Kong-style local cafes) and yum cha restaurants are already busy preparing an incredible array of food for breakfasts.

The choices are plentiful, depending on what kind of food you feel like, or how much time you have.

Want something clean? You've got congee and rice noodle roll, washed down with a refreshing glass of fresh soy milk. Want something Western? The numerous cha chaan teng around the city have sandwiches filled with scrambled eggs or corned beef and egg, plus pineapple buns with butter – or even satay beef with instant noodles – and a hot cup of Hong Kong signature milk tea.

PEARL TEA

EGG WAFFLE

EGG TART

BAG NOODLES

Do you have plenty of time and are looking for variety? Go yum cha and select whatever dim sum you like. Or are you rushing to get to work and have no time? Grab a sticky rice roll or a custardy egg tart.

While most of these offerings are now most commonly found in the more permanent stores and restaurants, you could still find some of them sold in the handful of *dai pai dong* (streetside food carts) left in the city. Look for them in Sham Shui Po (Kowloon) and Central (Hong Kong Island).

HONG KONG JUK

Congee (or *juk* in Cantonese) is a beloved staple across Asia and remains a traditional breakfast for Chinese people living all over the world.

Despite its long history and association with Chinese cuisine, it's believed that congee originated in ancient India and spread throughout Asia due to Portuguese traders.

Depending on local culture, congee varies in texture, ingredients used, toppings and cooking methods. For example, Hong Kong-style congee tends to be starchy, smooth and fluffy, a texture that should quickly melt in your mouth. Signature Hong Kong-style congee include *pei daan sau yuk juk* (congee with century egg and lean meat) and *teng zai juk* (sampan/boat congee).

Another popular variety in Hong Kong is Chiu Chow-style congee, which is a little more soup-like and uses seafood such as oyster and fish. A signature dish includes *ho zai juk* (baby oyster congee).

Hong Kong people love hotpot, especially in winter, so much so they've even combined it with congee. Often called porridge hotpot, the base is a thick congee flavoured with rich broth, such as crab, and served with an array of toppings and condiments – eveything from lobster, crispy fish skin and truffle, to pork and beef slices and beancurd.

JUK

Basic congee

Congee is often thought of as a flavourless bowl of rice eaten when you're not feeling well. In fact, congee is quite magical, it just needs to be made correctly. As simple as it sounds, cooking a bowl of silky and soul-satisfying congee requires a high level of attention and care.

Hong Kong-style congee is different from other regions, both in the way it is cooked (the method is called *san gwan*) and the versatility of its ingredients. Some people eat it with side dishes such as *yau ja gwai* (Chinese doughnut), *cheung fun* (rice noodle roll) or *chow mein* (stir-fried noodles), but it also tastes great served simply with a bit of salt!

Today, congee is mainly sold in stores (as opposed to prepared at home) and may be enjoyed at any time of the day).

Serves 8

100 g (3½ oz/½ cup) jasmine rice

1 Wash the rice, then drain and put it in the freezer for at least 8 hours. (If you don't have time, you can skip this step but it reduces the cooking time and results in a silkier texture.)

2 Combine the rice and 2.5 litres (2½ quarts) water in a large saucepan and bring to the boil over high heat, stirring constantly to prevent the rice from sticking to the bottom. Reduce the heat and simmer for 1 hour or until the rice has broken down and the congee has thickened, stirring occasionally to prevent sticking. (If the rice hasn't been in the freezer, the cooking time will be about 3 hours.)

3 Ladle the congee into bowls to serve. Season with a pinch of salt and white pepper if you're eating it plain.

PEI DAN SAU YUK JUK

Congee with lean pork and century egg

This is probably one of the most popular congee combinations eaten by Hongkongers at breakfast time. It is best known for its nutritional benefit of 'reducing the heat' inside your body: calming the stomach and aiding digestion.

Century eggs (or thousand-year eggs) are a Chinese delicacy made of preserved duck eggs – but don't worry, they're not actually preserved for a hundred (or a thousand!) years. The process usually takes a few weeks, maybe a few moths. They have a creamy texture and slight ammonia flavour on the inside and a blackish, transparent, jelly-like texture on the outside. They're an acquired taste – normal to me, because I grew up in Hong Kong – but for those who haven't tried them before, this congee is a great introduction to the century egg's unique taste.

Serves 2

200 g (7 oz) lean pork fillet, cut into thin strips

fine sea salt and white pepper

500 g (1 lb 2 oz/2 cups) Basic congee (page 13)

1 century egg, cut into 8 pieces

30 g (1 oz/½ cup) chopped spring (green) onion, white and green parts

4 slices ginger, julienned

½ teaspoon ground white pepper

1 Season the pork with a pinch each of salt and pepper. Cover and set aside in the fridge for 2 hours.

2 Pour the congee into a medium saucepan and heat over medium heat until hot. Add the pork and cook for 5 minutes, then reduce the heat to low. Add the century egg and cook for another 5 minutes.

3 Ladle into bowls, garnish with the spring onion, ginger and more white pepper and serve.

NGAU LEI SO

Sweet Chinese doughnuts

Chinese doughnuts are a golden-brown strip of dough, which make a perfect accompaniment to congee or fresh soy milk for breakfast in Hong Kong. While the savoury Chinese doughnuts are more well known around the world, this recipe is for the sweet version, *ngau lei so*, which literally translated from Cantonese means 'ox tongue pastry' as it is kind of looks like the shape of an ox tongue!

Makes 10

2 litres (2 quarts) canola oil (or other cooking oil)

Starter

125 g (4½ oz) plain (all-purpose) flour

icing (confectioners') sugar, for dusting

Water pastry

55 g (2 oz) caster (superfine) sugar

¼ teaspoon baking soda

¼ teaspoon salt

⅛ teaspoon alkaline water (see Notes)

90 g (3 oz) starter

150 g (5½ oz/1 cup) cake flour

150 g (5½ oz/1 cup) bread flour

Oil pastry

100 g (3½ oz) caster (superfine) sugar

⅛ teaspoon baking soda

1 tablespoon vegetable oil

25 g (1 oz) starter

180 g (6½ oz) cake flour

1 To make the starter, mix together 100 g (3½ oz/⅔ cup) of the flour and 100 ml (3½ fl oz) tepid water. Place in a clean container, cover and leave to ferment at room temperature for 1 day. Feed with 25 g (1 oz) flour mixed with 25 ml (1 fl oz) water, cover and leave for another day.

2 To make the water pastry, place the sugar in a large bowl, add 160 ml (5½ fl oz) tepid water and stir until dissolved. Add the baking soda, salt, alkaline water and starter and mix well, then add the flours and mix to form a dough. Mix in the bowl for 10 minutes (or use a stand mixer fitted with a dough hook). The dough will still be quite sticky at this stage. Cover and rest in the bowl for 10 minutes. Turn out onto a clean bench and knead the dough for a further 5–10 minutes. Cover with plastic wrap and rest for 15 minutes.

3 Roll the dough into a square about 3 cm (1¼ in) thick, fold in half from left to right, then fold in half again from top to bottom. Cover with plastic wrap and rest for another 30 minutes.

4 Meanwhile, prepare the oil pastry. Dissolve the sugar in 65 ml (2¼ fl oz) tepid water, then add the baking soda and oil and mix well. Add the starter and cake flour and stir until combined. Cover and rest for 10 minutes. Knead in the bowl for 5 minutes, then turn out onto a clean bench and knead for another 10 minutes, sprinkling with more flour if necessary. Cover with plastic wrap and rest for 15 minutes.

5 On a lightly floured surface, roll out the water pastry to a 30 cm (11¾ in) square. Roll out the oil pastry to a 30 cm x 15 cm (12 in x 6 in) rectangle.

6 Position the oil pastry on top of the water pastry (in the middle), then pinch down the edges of the oil pastry to secure it to the water pastry.

7 Fold the water pastry over the two long sides of the oil pastry and pinch the meeting point to secure. You should now have one 30 cm x 15 cm (12 in x 6 in) rectangle, about 2.5 cm (1 in) in height. Position the dough with the longest side closest to you, then cut into ten 15 cm x 3 cm (6 in x 1¼ in) strips.

8 Turn all the strips on their sides so the cut sides face up, then, if necessary, gently roll so the strips are all similar in height.

9 Pour the oil into a large wok and heat over high heat until it reaches 160°C (320°F) or until a cube of bread dropped in the oil browns in 30–35 seconds. Reduce the heat to medium.

10 Working in batches of three or four at a time, add the dough strips and cook for 1 minute each side. Keep turning and frying for another 4–5 minutes until the dough has puffed up and is golden brown. Remove with a slotted spoon and drain on paper towel. Dust with icing sugar and serve the doughnuts warm. Will keep in an airtight container for up to 2 days.

Notes

Alkaline water, sometimes sold as lye water, is available in Asian supermarkets.

This is not an easy recipe so don't be discouraged if it doesn't turn out the way you want it first time – practice makes perfect! Learn from your mistakes and try again.

Sweet Chinese doughnuts, page 16.

FRESH SOY MILK

If you happen to visit Hong Kong during the summer, there's no better way to begin your morning than with a cold and slightly sweetened fresh soy milk!

Makes 1 litre (1 quart/4 cups)

500 g (1 lb 2 oz) organic dried soy beans (see Note)

fine sea salt or caster (superfine) sugar, to taste

1 Soak the soy beans in a large bowl of water overnight. Drain.

2 Transfer the soy beans to a large saucepan and add 3 litres (3 quarts) water. Bring to the boil, then reduce the heat simmer for about 20 minutes or until the beans are soft enough to blend.

3 Using a stick blender, blend the beans and cooking water until smooth, then simmer over low heat for another 30–45 minutes. The time varies according to whether you like your soy milk thin or quite thick – the longer you cook it, the thicker it becomes.

4 Strain through a fine sieve lined with muslin (cheesecloth), then season to taste with salt or sugar. Transfer to a clean jug or bottle and chill before drinking. Fresh soy milk will keep in the fridge for up to 1 week.

Note

You can buy dried soy beans in Asian supermarkets. You may need to head to a health food store to find the organic ones.

CHA CHAAN TENG

A morning in Hong Kong isn't complete without a visit to a *cha chaan teng* (a Hong Kong-style local café) and a *dai pai dong* (a streetside food stall) to sample authentic Hong Kong-style breakfasts with Western influence.

Back in the colonial times, dining in Western restaurants was only for the upper class and Western cuisine was still a luxury to ordinary people. As incomes rose (along with the influence of British culture), cha chaan teng (Cantonese for 'tea restaurant') started popping up all over the city. An East-meets-West concept that was created in the 1950s, cha chaan tengs have popularised a distinctly local and comforting fusion of Cantonese cuisine and Western diner food.

While every place is different and the menus offer an extraordinary amount of choice, iconic cha chaan teng dishes include HK-style French toast with maple syrup or condensed milk (often filled with peanut butter or kaya jam); macaroni in soup with

ham; pineapple buns filled with slabs of cold salted butter; scrambled eggs on fluffy white toast or stuffed into a sandwich with slices of beef; instant noodles topped with Spam or satay beef. All are washed down with a hot cup of the signature Hong Kong milk tea or *yuenyueng*, a mixture of coffee and milk tea.

Cha chaan teng have always been popular for their convenience (they can be found *everywhere* in Hong Kong), flexibility (you can order pretty much any food combination you wish) and efficiency (the service is famously fast). However, do not expect quality service unless you're a regular customer!

MILK TEA

KONG SIK NAI CHA

Hong Kong-style milk tea

Unlike a lot of countries with a strong coffee culture, the people of Hong Kong focus on tea made with evaporated milk. Some industry statistics report that Hongkongers consume about 1 billion cups each year. So what is so special about this milk tea?

Influenced by British afternoon tea, this East-meets-West in a drink is also called *si mat lai cha* or 'silk-stocking milk tea' as it is made by repeatedly straining the tea through a very fine cloth; in the process the cloth turns brown, taking on the appearance of a silk stocking. In addition to the technique, the use of Black & White evaporated milk (imported from Holland and the only brand Hong Kong *cha chaan teng* use) makes this rendition of milk tea particularly rich and fragrant.

If you are a coffee lover, try a cup of *yuenyueng* – coffee mixed with milk tea.

Serves 4

5 English Breakfast tea bags

5 Ceylon Orange Pekoe tea bags

3 Earl Grey tea bags

300 ml (10 fl oz) evaporated milk (preferably Black & White brand)

100 g (3½ oz) caster (superfine) sugar, or to taste

1 Pour 1.5 litres (1½ quarts) water into a medium saucepan and bring to the boil over high heat. Add the tea bags, then reduce the heat and simmer for 20 minutes. Remove from the heat, cover and set aside for 10 minutes.

2 If you want to go all out, strain the tea from a height through a fine cloth a few times. (Traditionally you strain it from a height so the water pressure extracts more of the tea flavour, while the fine cloth catches the tannins and impurities.)

3 Pour evaporated milk into each cup until it is one-quarter full, then pour in the tea (the golden ratio is one part evaporated milk to three parts tea). Add sugar to taste and enjoy the moment.

CHI FAN

Sticky rice roll with Chinese doughnut and pork floss

Sticky rice roll is a popular dish of Shanghai origin. Here it is filled with a combination of crispy savoury Chinese doughnut and pork floss, with chopped preserved vegetables in between for their umami flavour. It's like a sticky, warm version of sushi. In winter, a freshly made sticky rice roll can be used as a 'hand warmer' while you're enjoying it!

Serves 4

500 g (1 lb 2 oz/2½ cups) glutinous rice, washed and soaked overnight in cold water

100 g (3½ oz) preserved or pickled vegetables

1 litre (1 quart/4 cups) canola oil (or other cooking oil)

1 store-bought savoury Chinese doughnut

50 g (1¾ oz) pork floss

1 Pour water into a large saucepan to a depth of about 3 cm (1¼ in) and bring to the boil. Line a bamboo basket or a sieve with muslin (cheesecloth) – choose one that can sit inside the pan without touching the water.

2 Add the rice and spread it out evenly, then make a little hole in the middle (this will help the steam to come through and ensure the rice is cooked properly). Cover and steam for 25–30 minutes until the rice is tender.

3 If you are using a packet of ready-to-eat preserved vegetables, just give them a rough chop. If you are using whole preserved vegetables, you might need to give them a rinse or even a soak before chopping, depending on how salty they are.

4 Pour the oil into a medium saucepan and heat to 170°C (340°F) or until a cube of bread dropped in the oil browns in 20 seconds. Add the Chinese doughnut and fry for about 1 minute, turning constantly, to give it a crunchier texture. Remove with tongs and drain on paper towel. Alternatively, preheat the oven to 180°C (350°F) and heat the Chinese doughnut up for 2 minutes.

5 Split the Chinese doughnut in half lengthways, then cut each piece in half, or into 12 cm (4¾ in) lengths.

6 Lay a cloth or a sushi mat on the table, then a piece of plastic wrap (about 25 cm x 25 cm/10 in x 10 in). Spread one-quarter of the rice over the plastic wrap in a rectangle as if you were making a sushi roll.

7 Arrange the pork floss lengthways in the centre of the rectangle. Top with the preserved vegetables, then the Chinese doughnut. Using the cloth or sushi mat, roll up the rice to enclose the filling and make a firm roll. Hold and twist both ends of the plastic wrap in opposite directions to tighten the roll and press firmly to seal. Repeat with the remaining ingredients to make four rolls in total.

8 Rest for about 10 minutes. These rolls are traditionally eaten whole, like a kebab, so you can keep the plastic and unwrap it as you eat. Alternatively, you can unwrap it and cut it into pieces.

SA CHA BEEF NOODLES

In Hong Kong this dish is known as satay, but it's not like the Thai-style satay made with peanuts and turmeric. Hong Kong-style satay sauce (also called sa cha sauce) is dark brown in colour and less spicy. Though not a fancy dish, a bowl of this is one of the most popular things to order in a Hong Kong-style cafe.

Serves 4

300 g (10½ oz) beef tenderloin (or any cut for quick-cooking), cut into thin strips

100 g (3½ oz/⅓ cup) sa cha sauce (see Notes)

1 teaspoon caster (superfine) sugar

3 tablespoons canola oil (or other cooking oil)

1 garlic clove, finely chopped

1 red shallot, finely chopped

340 g (12 oz) instant noodles

sliced spring (green onion) to serve

toasted sesame seeds, to serve

Marinade

1 tablespoon light soy sauce

1 teaspoon caster (superfine) sugar

2 teaspoons cornflour (cornstarch)

1 tablespoon canola oil

1 To make the marinade, combine all the ingredients and 2 tablespoons water in a bowl. Add the beef and turn to coat well, then set aside to marinate for 30 minutes.

2 In a small bowl, combine the sa cha sauce, sugar and 125 ml (4 fl oz/½ cup) water.

3 Heat a frying pan over high heat. Add 1 tablespoon oil, then the beef and saute for 2 minutes until almost cooked and just starting to brown. Transfer the beef to a bowl and set aside. Wipe out the pan and return to high heat. Heat the remaining oil, then add the garlic and shallot and saute for 30 seconds. Add the beef, followed by the sauce mixture. Reduce the heat to low and cook for about 2 minutes, or until heated through and the beef has had time to absorb the flavour.

4 Meanwhile, cook the noodles according to the packet instructions. Drain.

5 Divide the noodles among serving bowls and top with the beef and sauce and sprinkle with spring onion and sesame seeds.

Notes

For a healthier version, use rice vermicelli instead of instant noodles.

Sa cha sauce is available in Asian grocery stores.

YUM CHA AND DIM SUM

Yum cha literally means 'drink tea' in Cantonese, in reference to the plentiful pots consumed in order to aid digestion during this time-honoured *dim sum* (which means 'touch the heart') eating ritual. Yum cha has a long history and is believed to have first appeared in China during the Tang Dynasty (618–907 CE).

Essentially the practice of eating a range of dim sum accompanied by the eponymous tea, yum cha has undergone a significant evolution in the past few decades – from staff carrying pre-cooked dim sum in big baskets in the 1960s, changing to the use of dim sum push-carts or trolleys (for more choice and quantity in one go) and the eventual adoption of a paper-based ordering system allowing for made-to-order demand and the reduction of food wastage now used in most dim sum restaurants.

Today, yum cha comes in many different shapes and sizes, with restaurants usually either choosing a traditional approach or embracing innovation with the inclusion of new ingredients such as truffles and putting modern twists on their presentation, such as dumplings shaped like animal faces.

Usually eaten early in the day, with most restaurants offering 11 am or 1 pm sittings, going for yum cha remains an important social and culinary ritual for Hong Kong people and a fantastic meal to share with family and friends.

Since the charm of yum cha is in the variety, there's no right or wrong way to order – but a good way to judge a yum cha place is by the quality of their *har gow* (shrimp dumplings) and *siu mai* (pork and mushroom dumplings). Other classics to try are steamed pork ribs with black bean and chilli, steamed glutinous rice in lotus leaf, *cheung fan* (rice noodle stuffed with prawns or char siu pork) and steamed Malay sponge cake. And if you find yourself in a more modern yum cha restaurant, look for baked barbecue pork buns and runny egg yolk custard buns.

SIU MAI

Pork and mushroom dumplings

Before being introduced to Hong Kong, the earliest appearance of these dumplings dates back to 13th century China. Quite different from *har gow*, which is an elegant dumpling, *siu mai* (pictured on page 39) is an open-topped meaty dim sum that is comforting and filling. Both varieties are often served together and are the 'twins' on every dim sum menu! Other fillings include fish paste, beef and pork liver, but pork and mushroom is definitely the classic.

Makes 15–20

8 pieces dried shiitake mushroom

200 g (7 oz) peeled, deveined prawns (shrimp)

¾ teaspoon fine sea salt

50 g (1¾ oz) pork fat, finely diced

225 g (8 oz) pork loin, finely diced

1 tablespoon light soy sauce

1 tablespoon chopped spring (green) onion, white part only

2 teaspoons shaoxing rice wine

⅛ teaspoon ground white pepper

1 teaspoon caster (superfine) sugar

2 teaspoons sesame oil

2 teaspoons cornflour (cornstarch)

15–20 yellow wonton wrappers

1 Soak the dried shiitake in tepid water for 6 hours or overnight. Remove the stem, then squeeze out any excess water and finely dice.

2 Toss the prawns with ½ teaspoon salt, then rinse under cold running water and pat dry with paper towel. Store in the fridge for 1 hour, then finely dice.

3 Cook the pork fat in boiling water for 5–10 minutes until transparent. Rinse under cold running water until cool, then pat dry.

4 Mix together the pork loin, soy sauce and remaining salt; keep stirring until it becomes sticky. Lift the mixture and slap it back into the bowl five or six times to make it more elastic. Stir in the prawn meat and slap the mixture another five or six times.

5 Add the shiitake, pork fat, spring onion, shaoxing wine, pepper, sugar, sesame oil and cornflour and mix until well combined. Transfer to the fridge and chill for 20 minutes.

6 Hold a wonton wrapper in one hand and spoon 1 heaped tablespoon of the pork mixture into the middle. Working your way around the filling, push the wonton wrapper up so that it is wrapped around the filling, leaving the top part exposed. Place the dumpling in a steamer or on a plate. Repeat with the remaining wrappers and filling.

7 Pour water into a large saucepan to a depth of about 3 cm (1¼ in) and bring to the boil. Cover and steam the dumplings for 6–8 minutes. Depending on the size of your steamer you may need to do this in two batches. Serve hot.

HAR GOW

Shrimp dumplings

If you're travelling to Hong Kong in a group, yum cha is probably one of the best dining options for you and your companions, offering both authenticity and variety. *Har gow* (pictured on page 39) remains one of the four key dim sum at yum cha restaurants. Originally from Guangdong, China, it was Hong Kong that brought it into the international food arena.

Dumplings can be boiled, steamed or fried. Har gow is a steamed dumpling with a skin made of a hot water wheat starch dough, which becomes softly transparent when cooked. These dumplings are considered a test for the skill of a great dim sum chef!

Makes 24–30

420 g (15 oz) peeled, deveined prawns (shrimp)

1¼ teaspoons fine sea salt

½ teaspoon caster (superfine) sugar

⅛ teaspoon ground white pepper

2 teaspoons sesame oil

2 teaspoons canola oil

70 g (2½ oz) pork fat, thinly sliced

100 g (3½ oz) bamboo shoots

Dumpling skins

200 g (7 oz/1 cup) wheat starch

½ teaspoon fine sea salt

250 ml (8½ fl oz/1 cup) boiling water

2 tablespoons cornflour (cornstarch)

1 tablespoon lard

1 Toss the prawns with ½ teaspoon of the salt, give them a quick rub, then rinse under cold running water and pat dry with paper towel. Store in the fridge for 2 hours. Place half the prawns into a mixing bowl. Finely chop the remaining prawns and add to the bowl along with the salt. Using a clean hand, mix in one direction using a circular motion until the mixture is elastic. Add the sugar, white pepper, sesame oil and canola oil and gently combine.

2 Bring a small saucepan of water to the boil over high heat. Add the pork fat and bring back to the boil. Immediately drain and rinse the pork fat in cold running water. Pat dry with paper towel. Squeeze out any excess water, then finely dice the pork fat. Repeat this process to blanch the bamboo shoots.

3 Combine the pork fat, bamboo shoots and prawn meat and set aside in the fridge.

4 To make the dumpling skins, combine the wheat starch and salt in a mixing bowl. Pour in the boiling water and mix well with a pair of chopsticks or a spoon. Cover with plastic wrap and rest for 5 minutes. Add the cornflour and lard, then knead the dough until smooth and well combined.

5 Divide the dough into four pieces. Work with one portion at a time and keep the rest covered with a clean damp cloth to stop the dough drying out. Roll one piece of dough into a long cylinder about 2 cm (¾ in) thick, then cut into six or seven 1.5 cm (½ in) pieces.

6 If you are feeling adventurous you could use a flat cleaver to flatten the dough, like a professional dim sum chef does. Otherwise a rolling pin will do. Just make sure you work quickly; if the dough starts to crack it means it is too dry, which will make it very difficult to fold and the finished texture will be rubbery.

7 Roll each piece of dough into a 7 cm (2¾ in) circle and lightly oil each one.

8 Pick up a round of dough with your left hand, oil side down, and add a teaspoon of the filling. Pleat the dumpling by pushing the dumpling skin with the index finger of one hand and pressing to secure the pleat with the index finger of the other hand. You should be able to achieve 7–8 pleats. If this is too tricky, simply seal the dumpling however you wish – they may not look traditional but they'll still taste great.

9 Repeat with the remaining dough and filling, covering the dumplings as you make them so they don't dry out.

10 Pour water into a large saucepan to a depth of about 3 cm (1¼ in) and bring to the boil. Lightly oil a large bamboo steamer to prevent sticking and line with baking paper or individual dim sum papers.

11 Working in batches, add the dumplings to the steamer basket in a single layer, then cover and steam for 3–4 minutes or until soft and translucent. Remove from the heat and rest for 1 minute before opening the lid. Serve hot.

Clockwise from above: Pork and cabbage dumplings, page 40; Har gow, page 36; Siu mai, page 35.

PORK AND CABBAGE DUMPLINGS

These are another staple on the yum cha trolley, and probably one of the most well-known and widely enjoyed Chinese foods among Westerners. Who doesn't love a good pork and cabbage dumpling (pictured on page 38)? Aside from the countless yum cha restaurants, Hong Kong is also full of stores selling high-quality pre-made dumplings from many different regions for locals to cook at home.

Makes about 40

6 dried shiitake mushrooms

2 tablespoons dried shrimp

285 g (10 oz) wombok (Chinese cabbage), finely chopped

2 teaspoons fine sea salt

2 tablespoons canola oil

225 g (8 oz) minced (ground) pork

2 tablespoons light soy sauce

1 teaspoon minced ginger

1 teaspoon caster (superfine) sugar

1 tablespoon shaoxing rice wine

1 tablespoon sesame oil

⅛ teaspoon ground white pepper

30 g (1 oz) finely chopped spring (green) onion

Dumpling dipping sauce (page 144), to serve

Dumpling skins

200 g (7 oz/1⅓ cups) bread flour

100 g (3½ oz/⅔ cup) plain (all-purpose) flour

1 teaspoon fine sea salt

1 Soak the dried shiitake in 250 ml (8½ fl oz/1 cup) water for at least 8 hours or overnight. Strain and reserve the liquid. Soak the dried shrimp in 3 tablespoons water for 30 minutes. Finely dice the shrimp and shiitake.

2 Mix the cabbage and 1 teaspoon of the salt, then set aside for 30 minutes or until soft. Drain and squeeze out any excess water from the cabbage.

3 Heat the canola oil in a large frying pan over high heat, add the shrimp and shiitake and saute for 2–3 minutes until fragrant.

4 Mix the pork with the remaining salt and the soy sauce, stirring until sticky, then gradually add up to 3 tablespoons of the reserved shiitake soaking liquid. Continue mixing until the meat mixture has absorbed all the liquid. Add the ginger, sugar, shaoxing wine, sesame oil, pepper and spring onion, then add the cabbage and mix well. Store in the fridge for at least 3 hours to give the flavours time to develop.

5 To make the dumpling skins, combine the flours and salt in a bowl, then add 180–200 ml (6–7 fl oz) tepid water and mix until well combined. Knead in the bowl for about 5 minutes.

6 Turn out onto a clean bench (no need to flour the bench even if the dough feels slightly sticky). Knead the dough by pushing it away and rolling it back, then turning it 90 degrees, pushing away and rolling back, and so on, for another 5 minutes. Roll the dough into a ball, cover with plastic wrap and rest for 15 minutes.

7 After resting, knead the dough again as you would knead bread (push in, turn, push in, turn) for another 5 minutes. The dough should now be nice and smooth. Roll the dough into a ball, cover with plastic wrap and rest for another 30 minutes.

8 Roll the dough into four cylinders and cut each cylinder into 10 even-sized pieces. Roll each piece into a thin round. Cover the rolled-out skins with a clean damp cloth so they don't dry out.

9 Pick up a round of dough with your left hand, dampen the edge with a little water and add a teaspoon of the filling. Pleat the dumpling by pushing the dumpling skin with the index finger of one hand and pressing to secure the pleat with the index finger of the other hand. You should be able to achieve 7–8 pleats. If this is too tricky, simply seal the dumplings however you wish – they may not look traditional but they'll still taste great.

10 Repeat with the remaining dough and filling, covering the dumplings as you make them so they don't dry out.

11 Pour water into a large saucepan to a depth of about 3 cm (1¼ in) and bring to the boil. Lightly oil a large bamboo steamer to prevent sticking and line with baking paper or individual dim sum papers.

12 Working in batches, add the dumplings to the steamer in a single layer, then cover and steam for 6–8 minutes or until cooked through. Serve hot with dumpling dipping sauce.

LO MAI GAI

Sticky rice with chicken in lotus leaf

In this classic dim sum, marinated chicken, shiitake, salted egg yolk and glutinous rice are wrapped in lotus leaf and steamed. The portion size is quite large, making it rather heavy and filling; however, there is a smaller variant (*chun chu gai*) for those who want to try a variety of dim sum. I give the traditional filling here but by all means make your own version with your favourite kind of meat and vegetables.

Makes 4

400 g (14 oz/2 cups) glutinous rice

2 dried shiitake mushrooms

1 teaspoon lard

½ teaspoon fine sea salt

50 g (1¾ oz) bamboo shoots, finely diced

150 g (5½ oz) boneless, skinless chicken thighs, sliced

100 g (3½ oz) pork collar butt (preferably with about 30% fat content), sliced

3 tablespoons canola oil (or other cooking oil)

1 teaspoon crushed garlic

2 thin slices ginger

1 teaspoon shaoxing rice wine

3 dried lotus leaves (see glossary)

2 salted duck egg yolks, halved (see glossary)

Marinade

¼ teaspoon fine sea salt

½ teaspoon caster (superfine) sugar

½ teaspoon light soy sauce

⅛ teaspoon ground white pepper

¼ teaspoon shaoxing rice wine

⅛ teaspoon cornflour (cornstarch)

Sauce

1 tablespoon oyster sauce

1 teaspoon light soy sauce

¼ teaspoon caster (superfine) sugar

⅛ teaspoon ground white pepper

⅛ teaspoon sesame oil

1 teaspoon cornflour (cornstarch)

1 Wash the rice and soak in water overnight.

2 Soak the dried shiitake in 250 ml (8½ fl oz/1 cup) tepid water for 6 hours or overnight. Drain, then finely dice.

3 Drain the rice and mix in the lard and salt. Pour water into a large saucepan to a depth of about 3 cm (1¼ in) and bring to the boil. Arrange the rice mixture on a steamer tray or plate, then cover and steam for 30 minutes or until tender.

4 Blanch the shiitake and bamboo shoot in boiling water for 30 seconds. Drain and refresh under cold running water.

5 To make the marinade, combine all the ingredients in a bowl. Add the chicken and pork and turn to coat well, then set aside for 30 minutes.

6 Heat 1 tablespoon of the oil in a large frying pan over high heat, add the chicken and pork and cook for 2 minutes or until browned. Remove from the pan and set aside.

7 To make the sauce, combine all the ingredients and 80 ml (2½ fl oz/⅓ cup) water in a bowl. Add to the pan and cook, stirring, over medium–high heat for 30 seconds or until the sauce has thickened. Set aside to cool.

8 Wipe out the pan, add the remaining oil and place over medium heat. Add the garlic and ginger and saute for 10 seconds or until fragrant. Add the shiitake and bamboo shoot and saute for 30 seconds. Deglaze the pan with shaoxing wine. Return the chicken and pork to the pan and cook for another 30 seconds, then add the sauce and cook for another 30 seconds.

9 Blanch the lotus leaves in boiling water for 10 seconds, then rinse under cold running water and pat dry. Cut each leaf in half, and spread on a clean bench. If necessary, wipe again with paper towel to ensure the leaves are completely dry.

10 Place two leaves on top of each other to form a double layer. Put a thin layer of rice in the centre of the stacked leaves, then top with a quarter of the chicken and pork mixture and a piece of salted duck egg yolk. Cover with another layer of rice, then fold in the sides of the leaf and wrap up to enclose the filling. Repeat with the remaining leaves and filling.

11 Pour water into a large saucepan to a depth of about 3 cm (1¼ in) and bring to the boil. Arrange the lotus leaf parcels on a steamer tray or plate (without overlapping), then cover and steam for 15 minutes. Unwrap the lotus leaf to eat.

CHING PAI KUAT
Steamed pork ribs

This is one of my favourite dim sum and I order it every time at yum cha. If you have never tried steamed pork ribs with preserved black beans and chopped chilli before, you may not be able to imagine how the flavours work but I promise you, they are delectable.

Serves 2–4

400 g (14 oz) pork ribs, cut into 2 cm (¾ in) cubes

2 tablespoons canola oil (or other cooking oil)

2 garlic cloves, chopped

2 teaspoons salted black beans

1 teaspoon cornflour (cornstarch)

½ teaspoon vegetable oil

thinly sliced red chilli, to garnish

Marinade

1 teaspoon fine sea salt

1 teaspoon caster (superfine) sugar

2 teaspoons shaoxing rice wine

¼ teaspoon baking soda

1 Soak the pork ribs in water for 15 minutes, then drain and replace with fresh water. Repeat the step about four times or until the pork meat has become quite pale because the blood has been released into the soaking water. Drain, pat dry with paper towel and place in a shallow bowl.

2 Combine the marinade ingredients together in a small bowl.

3 Heat the oil in a frying pan over medium–high heat, add the garlic and black beans and saute for 1 minute or until fragrant. Pour the mixture over the pork ribs, add the marinade and turn to coat well. Place in the fridge to marinate for 4 hours.

4 Blend the cornflour with 1 teaspoon water. Add the mixture to the pork ribs along with the vegetable oil and mix well.

5 Pour water into a large saucepan to a depth of about 3 cm (1¼ in) and bring to the boil. Arrange the pork ribs on a steamer tray or plate (without overlapping). Cover and steam for 15–20 minutes or until the pork is cooked through. Garnish with sliced chilli and serve.

CHEUNG FUN
Rice noodle roll

Originally from southern China, the silky rice noodle roll is a simple recipe that is hard to master as it only contains two main ingredients: rice flour and water. The thickness of the roll and smoothness of the texture are very much dependent on the skill of the chef. Rice noodle roll can be either plain or filled. A plain rice noodle roll is steamed in a thin layer and rolled up into a thick and chewy roll, often served with slightly sweetened soy sauce and toasted sesame seeds.

The rice noodle roll can also be made into a variety of dim sum, such as *ha cheung* (shrimp rice noodle roll), *ngau yuk cheung* (beef rice noodle roll), *char siu cheung* (barbecue pork rice noodle rice), *jar leung* (Chinese doughnut wrapped in rice noodle roll) and *chow cheung fun* (XO sauce stir-fry with rice noodle roll).

Serves 4

175 g (6 oz/1 cup) rice flour

1 tablespoon wheat starch

1 tablespoon tapioca starch

½ teaspoon fine sea salt

1 tablespoon canola oil (or other cooking oil)

toasted sesame seeds, to serve

Cheung fun sauce

2 tablespoons canola oil (or other cooking oil)

2 spring (green) onions, cut into 5 cm (2 in) lengths

2 slices ginger

2 coriander (cilantro) roots

10 g (¼ oz) yellow rock sugar

2 tablespoons light soy sauce

1 tablespoon dark soy sauce

1 Pour water into a large saucepan to a depth of about 3 cm (1¼ in) and bring to the boil. Add a steamer basket large enough to fit a 20 cm (7¾ in) square non-stick tin. Lightly grease the tin with oil, then place the saucepan over high heat to heat the tin.

2 Place the flour, starches, salt, oil and 500 ml (17 fl oz/2 cups) water in a bowl and stir well to combine. Ladle a little of the batter into the prepared tin, just enough to cover the base.

3 Cover and steam for 1–2 minutes or until cooked. Carefully remove the tin and gently roll the noodle from one end to the other.

4 Wipe the tin clean and lightly grease with oil. Repeat with the remaining batter, stirring it well each time. You should have enough to make about eight rolled noodles.

5 Meanwhile, to make the sauce, heat the oil in a medium saucepan over high heat, add the spring onion, ginger and coriander root and cook, stirring for 20 seconds or until fragrant. Add the rock sugar and 125 ml (4 fl oz/½ cup) water and bring to a simmer, stirring until the sugar has dissolved. Remove from the heat and stir in both soy sauces.

6 Serve the noodle rolls warm with the cheung fun sauce and sprinkled with toasted sesame seeds.

TONG

Tong (Cantonese for 'soup') is a classic symbol of the family meal. In Hong Kong, we have a saying, 'one soup, three dishes' (which is based on the Japanese principle called *ichiju-sansai*). Soup is believed to contain a lot of nutrients making it an essential part of any home-cooked meal.

Unlike in many Western countries where soup is often thickened by blending the ingredients, Hong Kong-style soup is usually more like a broth.

The different types of soup in Hong Kong can be categorised by cooking time:

1 'Boil from raw' soups take 15–20 minutes, often involving fresh and fast to cook ingredients like sliced fish or pork, with vegetables.

2 Standard soups normally take about 1–2 hours of cooking time.

3 'Old fire' soups (named *lou fo tong* in Cantonese, which means 'double-boiling soup' in English) take 3–4 hours, and include ingredients that require a little longer to extract the flavours, like tough chicken, or pork bones.

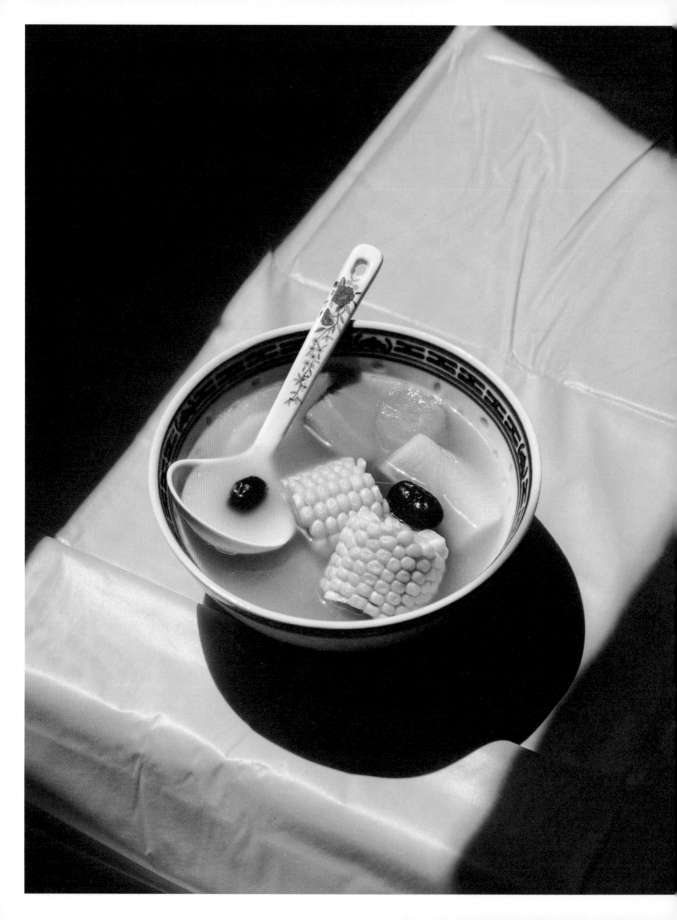

CARROT, DAIKON, CORN AND PORK SOUP

This is one of the easiest and most commonly made soups in Hong Kong kitchens. If you use organic carrots and daikon, you can just give the skin a really good wash and leave the skin on.

Serves 8

2 corn cobs, washed

1 kg (2 lb 3 oz) pork bones

2 carrots (about 600 g/1 lb 5 oz), peeled and cut into bite-sized pieces

400 g (14 oz) daikon, peeled and cut into bite-sized pieces

4 dried red dates (see glossary)

fine sea salt

1 Cut each corn cob into four or five pieces. You can keep the husk on if you wish – it will certainly contribute to the flavour.

2 Give the pork bones a good wash to remove any excess blood.

3 Put all the ingredients in a large saucepan, add 3 litres (3 quarts) water and bring to the boil over high heat, skimming off any impurities on the surface. Boil for 30 minutes, then reduce the heat to medium, cover with a lid and simmer for 2 hours. Remove from the heat and leave, covered, for another 30 minutes.

4 Season to taste with salt and ladle into bowls. You can eat the soup with the pork and vegetables left in, or just the broth by itself.

WUN JAI CHI

'Shark fin' soup

This dish mimics the expensive version of shark fin soup that used to be served at weddings and banquets in the old days. Over the years the real version has become less popular due to the increased concern about animal welfare and the damage associated with shark finning activities. Imitation shark fin soup originated in Hong Kong during the 1960s, offering an alternative for less affluent people at an affordable price. It remains popular to this day and is available from the road-side food stalls, fast-food stores and restaurants.

Serves 8

6 dried shiitake mushrooms

1 litre (1 quart/4 cups) chicken stock

150 g (5½ oz) lean pork loin or shoulder

150 g (5½ oz) boneless, skinless chicken breast

30 g (1 oz) dried black (woodear) fungus, soaked in water for 30 minutes

1 egg

60 g (2 oz) dried rice vermicelli, soaked in water for 15 minutes

1 tablespoon oyster sauce

1 tablespoon light soy sauce

1 teaspoon dark soy sauce

rice vinegar, ground white pepper and sesame oil, to serve

Slurry

1 tablespoon water chestnut flour (see Note)

1 tablespoon cornflour (cornstarch)

1 Soak the dried shiitake in 500 ml (17 fl oz/2 cups) tepid water for 6 hours or overnight. Remove the shiitake and reserve the soaking water. Strain it through a fine sieve to remove any dirt or sand.

2 Combine the chicken stock and reserved soaking liquid in a medium saucepan and add the pork, chicken breast and shiitake. Bring to the boil, then reduce the heat and simmer for 30 minutes or until the pork and chicken are cooked, skimming off any impurities on the surface.

3 Scoop out the pork, chicken and shiitake and set aside to cool, then finely slice them. Finely slice the rehydrated black fungus.

4 To make the slurry, combine the flours and 125 ml (4 fl oz/½ cup) water in a bowl.

5 Beat the egg in a bowl and add 1 tablespoon of the slurry.

6 Bring the stock back to the boil and add the sliced pork, chicken, shiitake and black fungus. Drain the vermicelli and stir into the soup, along with the oyster and soy sauces.

7 Reduce the heat to low and whisk in half the slurry. The soup will start to thicken slightly but you don't want it too thick. Add a little more slurry if it's still a bit watery.

8 Gently mix in the egg mixture and bring back to a simmer, then remove the soup from the heat.

9 Ladle into bowls and season to taste with rice vinegar, white pepper and sesame oil.

Note

Water chestnut flour is available from Asian supermarkets. If unavailable, you can use another tablespoon of cornflour (cornstarch) instead, but soup thickened with water chestnut flour will be more stable and less likely to split.

COCONUT AND CHICKEN SOUP

This slightly unusual soup is wonderfully easy to make. It's very clean and tasty with additional sweetness from the dried fruit and the clear coconut juice.

Serves 8

1 whole coconut

1.2 kg (2 lb 10 oz) whole chicken

300 g (10½ oz) pork shank (optional)

5 dried dates

2 dried figs

10 pieces dried whelk (see Note)

1 tablespoon goji berries

fine sea salt

1 Break the top part of the coconut with the back of a thick cleaver or a small hammer. Pour off the coconut water and reserve. Use a peeler or knife to remove the brown skin, then rinse the coconut meat and cut into bite-sized pieces.

2 Rinse the chicken and cut into chunks. Remove the skin if you like.

3 Pour 3 litres (3 quarts) water into a large saucepan and bring to the boil over high heat. Add the chicken and pork shank (if using) and boil for 1 minute, then remove the chicken and pork and give it a good rinse under cold running water. (This technique is used to remove the smell and blood from protein, giving a nice clean flavour.)

4 Drain and refill the pan with 4 litres (4 quarts) of fresh water. Add the chicken, pork, dates, figs, dried whelk, reserved coconut water and coconut meat. Bring to the boil and boil for 15 minutes, then reduce the heat to medium and simmer for 2 hours, skimming off impurities on the surface.

5 Remove from the heat, add the goji berries and leave, covered, for another 20 minutes. Season to taste with salt and serve.

Note
Look for dried whelk, whole or in slices, in the dried seafood section in your Asian supermaket. If unavailable, you can substitute dried scallop.

SAI DO SI
Hong Kong-style French toast

Hong Kong-style French toast is often made with savoury fillings, such as peanut butter, cheese or satay beef (I use kaya jam here, but feel free to use any flavour jam or other filling you might like). The bread is coated in egg and deep-fried (rather than pan-fried) and served with a generous amount of butter, maple syrup or condensed milk. My recipe here gives instructions for pan-frying, as it's easier to do at home, but do deep-fry if you wish. Paired with a cup of tea, this French toast is perfect for breakfast or at tea time.

Serves 2

4 slices soft white bread, crusts removed

1 tablespoon kaya jam (see glossary)

2 eggs

2 tablespoons milk

1 tablespoon vegetable oil

20 g (¾ oz) butter, plus extra to serve

maple syrup, to serve

1 Spread two slices of the bread with the kaya jam. Sandwich with the remaining bread and gently press to seal.

2 Whisk together the eggs and milk in a shallow bowl. Dip the sandwiches into the mixture to coat evenly.

3 Heat the oil and butter in a frying pan over medium heat. Add the coated sandwiches and fry for 1 minute each side or until golden brown, then stand the sandwich up and the edges for about 30 seconds each. Serve hot with extra butter and some maple syrup.

DAAN TAAT

Egg tarts

Egg tarts are a Western-influenced Cantonese dessert, which was first introduced into Hong Kong in the 1940s by chefs from Guangzhou, in southern China. Unlike the English or Portuguese custard tarts, this Cantonese pastry is traditionally made with lard rather than butter. The tart is filled with a soft, rich egg custard and can be made with two types of crusts: a flaky puff pastry crust or shortcrust pastry. The shortcrust is a little easier to make, so that's what I've done here, but each version has its own group of fans.

Makes 16

75 g (2¾ oz) caster (superfine) sugar

250 ml (8½ fl oz/1 cup) hot water

3 large eggs (and by this I mean 70 g/2½ oz eggs), at room temperature

125 ml (4 fl oz/½ cup) evaporated milk

½ teaspoon vanilla extract

Shortcrust pastry

60 g (2 oz) icing (confectioners') sugar

135 g (5 oz) unsalted butter, at room temperature

15 g (½ oz) beaten egg

200 g (7 oz/1⅓ cups) plain (all-purpose) flour

2½ tablespoons milk powder

1 Preheat the oven to 200°C (400°F). Lightly grease sixteen 5 cm (2 in) round tart tins.

2 To make the pastry, place the icing sugar and butter in a mixing bowl. Using your fingertips, rub the sugar into the butter. Work in the egg, followed by the flour and milk powder until the mixture is just combined (try not to overwork the dough). Wrap in plastic wrap and rest for 5 minutes in the fridge.

3 Roll out the dough into a cylinder shape on a lightly floured surface. Divide the dough into sixteen pieces (about 25 g/1 oz per piece), roll each piece into a ball and gently press out into 7 cm (2¾ in) rounds. Press the rounds into the prepared tins, pushing the dough slightly higher than the top edge. Place the tins on a tray, cover with plastic wrap and refrigerate for 30 minutes.

4 Place the sugar in a heatproof bowl, add the hot water and stir until the sugar has dissolved. Set aside to cool completely. In a separate bowl, lightly whisk the eggs, evaporated milk and vanilla – you just want to loosen the egg here so don't whisk too vigorously. Pour in the cooled sugar mixture and stir to combine, then gently strain through a fine sieve to get rid of any air bubbles.

5 Pour the custard into the tart shells until they are four-fifths full. Immediately place the tarts in the lower part of the oven (to help the pastry and custard cook at the same time) and bake for 15 minutes. Reduce the temperature to 180°C (350°F) and cook for another 5–10 minutes until the filling is just set. Serve warm. The tarts are best eaten on the day they're made, but can be stored in an airtight container and eaten the next day.

COCONUT TARTS

This is another popular tart that can be found in almost every Hong Kong-style bakery. Made with shortcrust pastry, this bakery treat has a wonderfully sweet fragrance from its sticky coconut filling. While egg tarts (page 59) can be a bit tricky for first timers, making coconut tarts is pretty easy! If you have left-over pastry from making egg tarts, by all means use it here.

Makes 16

60 g (2 oz) caster (superfine) sugar

90 g (3 oz/1 cup) shredded coconut

30 g (1 oz) unsalted butter

1 egg

1½ tablespoons evaporated milk

1 tablespoon cake flour

½ teaspoon baking powder

Shortcrust pastry

60 g (2 oz) icing (confectioners') sugar

135 g (5 oz) unsalted butter, at room temperature

15 g (½ oz) beaten egg

200 g (7 oz/1⅓ cups) plain (all-purpose) flour

2½ tablespoons milk powder

1 Preheat the oven to 200°C (400°F). Lightly grease sixteen 5 cm (2 in) round tart tins

2 To make the pastry, place the icing sugar and butter in a mixing bowl. Using your fingertips, rub the sugar into the butter. Work in the egg, followed by the flour and milk powder until the mixture is just combined (try not to overwork the dough). Wrap in plastic wrap and rest for 5 minutes in the fridge.

3 Roll out the dough into a cylinder shape on a lightly floured surface. Divide the dough into sixteen pieces (about 25 g/1 oz per piece), roll each piece into a ball and gently press out into 7 cm (2¾ in) rounds. Press the rounds into the prepared tins, pushing the dough slightly higher than the top edge. Place the tins on a tray, cover with plastic wrap and refrigerate for 30 minutes.

4 Pour 50 ml (1¾ fl oz) water into a small saucepan and bring to a simmer over high heat. Reduce the heat to medium, add the sugar and stir until dissolved. Add the desiccated coconut and cook for 3 minutes, then stir in the butter until melted and combined. Set aside to cool completely.

5 Whisk the egg and evaporated milk together, then mix into the cooled coconut mixture. Stir in the flour and baking powder.

6 Spoon 2 tablespoons filling into each tart shell (or pipe it in for a more professional finish). Bake for 15–20 minutes, then check them. If the filling is starting to turn golden brown but the pastry is not yet cooked, reduce the temperature to 180°C (350°F) and cook for another 5–10 minutes. Serve warm. Best eaten on the day they're made, but can be stored in an airtight container and eaten the next day.

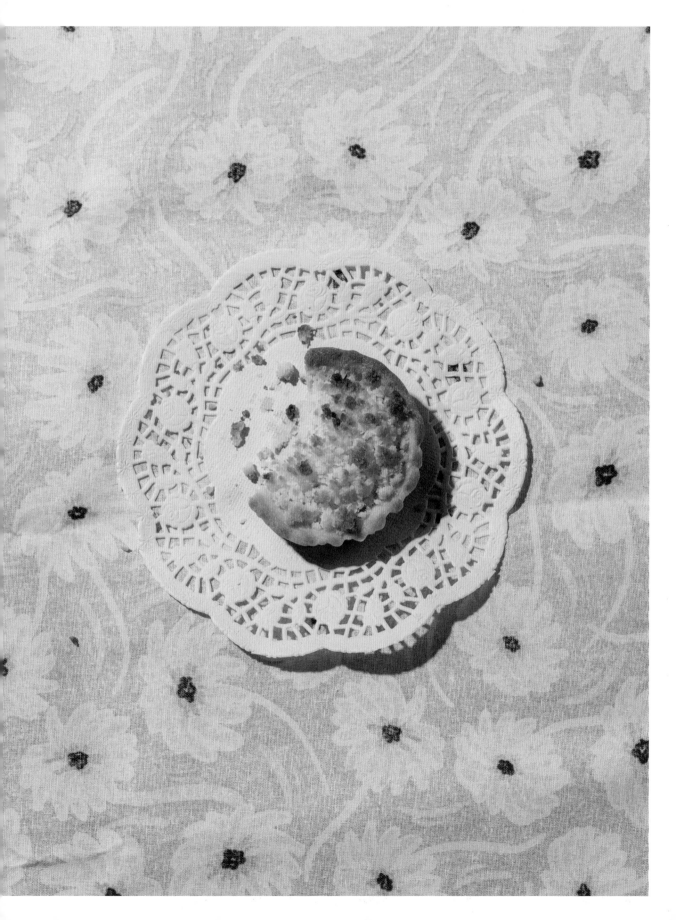

BO LO BAO

Pineapple bun with butter

Invented in Hong Kong in the 1960s, the pineapple bun is a traditional sweet snack, and a beloved treat for anyone of any age at any time of the day. There is no trace of pineapple in this bun – it gets its name from its golden crispy crust that looks a bit like a real pineapple, concealing a soft, fluffy centre. The slab of cold butter melting into the middle of a freshly baked bun is what makes these truly addictive. A true Hongkonger's favourite guilty pleasure!

Makes 8

1 egg yolk, lightly beaten

butter, to serve

Bun dough

60 g (2 oz) caster (superfine) sugar

5 g (¼ oz) instant dry yeast

1 egg, lightly beaten

2 teaspoons evaporated milk

60 g (2 oz) lard (or vegetable shortening) at room temperature

300 g (10½ oz/2 cups) bread flour

Pastry topping

¼ teaspoon baking soda

70 g (2½ oz) cake flour, plus extra for dusting

50 g (1¾ oz) icing (confectioners') sugar

1 egg yolk

1 teaspoon evaporated milk

30 g (1 oz) lard or vegetable shortening

1 To make the bun dough, combine the sugar, yeast and 150 ml (5 fl oz) tepid water in a bowl. Set aside for 5 minutes or until the mixture starts to bubble. Stir in the egg, evaporated milk and lard, then add the flour and gently mix until well combined.

2 Turn out the dough onto a clean surface and knead for 10 minutes. Cover with a clean damp cloth and rest for 10 minutes. Knead the dough for another 10 minutes or until smooth. Take a small piece of dough and do the 'windowpane' test: if you can stretch it relatively thinly without tearing it, that means the gluten has developed enough. If it tears, knead for a bit longer and try again.

3 Put the dough in a medium bowl, cover with a clean damp cloth and leave the dough to prove for 1–1½ hours or until it has nearly doubled in size. The proving time will depend on the temperature in the room – the warmer it is, the less time it will need.

4 Gently knock back the dough, then roll it into a cylinder for portioning. Divide the dough into eight even pieces and roll into balls. Place on a tray, cover with clean dry cloth and prove for an hour until doubled in size.

5 Preheat the oven to 200°C (400°F).

6 To make the topping, combine the baking soda, flour and sugar in a bowl. Add the egg, milk, lard and ½ teaspoon water and mix until just combined (do not overwork the dough). Cover the dough with plastic wrap and rest in the fridge for 30 minutes.

7 Cut the pastry topping into eight walnut-sized balls Lightly dust the surface with flour, then press down on each ball to form a thin disc. Place a disc on top of each bun.

8 Lightly spray the buns and topping with water, then brush the topping with the beaten egg yolk. Bake for about 15 minutes or until the buns are raised and golden brown. Cut in half and serve warm with a slice of good-quality butter. The buns are best eaten on the day they're made, but can be stored in an airtight container and eaten the next day.

MA LAI GO

Malay sponge cake

Some say this golden, airy sponge cake is originally from Malaysia, while others believe it was adapted from the British sponge cake by a Chinese chef who immigrated to colonial Malaysia. Whatever its origins, US news outlet CNN named it the national cake of Hong Kong. If you prefer a lighter alternative for sweet dim sum, this cake is definitely a good choice, especially when it is served steaming hot!

Serves 4

5 eggs

200 g (7 oz) brown sugar

200 ml (7 fl oz) evaporated milk

2½ tablespoons vegetable oil

6 g (¼ oz) instant dry yeast

200 g (7 oz/1⅓ cups) cake flour

3 tablespoons custard powder

2½ teaspoons baking powder

2½ tablespoons milk powder

1 Whisk the eggs and sugar together in a mixing bowl until fluffy. Add the evaporated milk and oil and mix gently. Sprinkle with the yeast and sift in the remaining ingredients. Gently fold in until combined. Set aside to rest at room temperature for 1 hour.

2 Line a 15 cm (6 in) steamer basket, about 5 cm (2 in) deep, with baking paper.

3 Pour the batter into the prepared tin (it should be about three-quarters full).

4 Pour water into a large saucepan to a depth of about 3 cm (1¼ in) and bring to the boil. Place the tin in a steamer basket, then cover and steam for 20–25 minutes until light and fluffy. Serve hot.

M

Mid

While there are plenty of lunch options in Hong Kong, locals are generally looking for something that's quick, filling and good value for money. That's why noodles (different types of noodles with meat, vegetables and soup) and rice dishes (usually rice with meat and vegetables on one plate) are very popular.

There are four common types of meal bases in Hong Kong: *juk* (congee), *fan* (steamed rice), *fun* (rice noodles) and *mein* (wheat noodles).

While congee is mainly eaten as a breakfast food, steamed rice is the overall main source of carbohydrates throughout the day – but noodles are the favourite for lunch.

Wonton mein (wonton noodles), *ngau lam mein* (braised beef brisket noodles) and *che jai mein* (cart noodles) are just a few of the most popular lunchtime noodle options.

Besides the range of local choices, Hongkongers love noodles from all over – you'll find plenty of variety including Vietnamese pho, Yunnan hot and sour noodle soup and fiery Sichuan mala noodles.

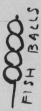

Hopefully you'll feel hungry a couple of hours after having lunch. When you do, it's time to try the street snacks, such as curry fish balls, three stuffed treasures (pan-fried fish paste stuffed with bell pepper/capsicum, fried tofu and eggplant), fake shark fin soup and more.

Feeling a bit tired after all the shopping? Find yourself a *cha chaan teng* (a Hong Kong-style local cafe) and rest your legs while enjoying a red bean and coconut shaved ice or an iced lemon tea. If you'd like a cup of milk tea, it's best enjoyed hot. You can get it chilled, but no place that's serious about their milk tea would serve it with ice in the actual drink, as it wouLd dilute the flavour.

And when you're ready for something sweet, look for the stores that specialise in milk and egg custards. Try a double-skin milk custard – you can get these hot or cold and they have a delicate milky flavour.

There are also plenty of dessert places that focus on local fruits. A signature Hong Kong combination is mango, sago, pomelo and coconut – a wonderful balance of flavour and texture.

SIU YUK

Crispy skin pork

Crispy skin pork or crispy pork belly is one of the best-known *siu mei* (barbecued meat dishes) in Hong Kong and around the world. There are a few ways to make the skin crispy and crunchy. The best way is to roast the pork over charcoal, but this is also very labour intensive and requires the chef to have extensive experience and superior skills. Here I use a simpler method and cook the pork in the oven. Try to buy pork belly with thin skin as this will give a much crisper crackling that isn't too hard.

Serves 8

70 g (2½ oz) fine sea salt

1.2 kg (2 lb 10 oz) boneless pork belly

Marinade

1 tablespoon fine sea salt

1 teaspoon caster (superfine) sugar

1 teaspoon Chinese five-spice

1 tablespoon roughly chopped garlic

4 cm (1½ in) piece ginger, roughly chopped

3–4 spring (green) onions, roughly chopped

1 tablespoon shaoxing rice wine

Skin

2 tablespoons vegetable oil

2 tablespoons fine sea salt

Sauce

1 tablespoon dijon mustard

1 tablespoon hoisin sauce

1 Dissolve the salt in 1.2 litres (1¼ quarts) water in a plastic container, then add the pork (you want it to be fully submerged) and set aside for 2 hours. Remove the pork and give it a quick rinse under water. Pat dry and scrape off any hair.

2 To make the marinade, mix all the ingredients together in a 30 cm x 25 cm (12 in x 10 in) baking tray. Place the pork belly on top of the marinade, meat side down. Pat the skin dry with paper towel, making sure none of the marinade touches it. Transfer the pork to the fridge and marinate, uncovered, for 24 hours to let the skin dry off.

3 Preheat the oven to 160°C (320°F).

4 To prepare the pork skin, rub the oil over the skin and sprinkle evenly with the salt.

5 Roast for 15 minutes, then increase the temperature to 180°C (350°F) and cook for a further 20 minutes. Crank up the oven to 250°C (480°F) or the highest possible temperature for a final 5–10 minutes, keeping an eye on the pork to ensure the skin doesn't burn – you want it to be golden and bubbling up to a nice crackling.

6 To make the sauce, mix together the mustard and hoisin sauce.

7 Remove the pork from the oven and rest for 20 minutes, then cut off the side and bottom of the pork, which will have dried out and blackened. Cut into pieces and serve with the sauce.

SIU MEI

Hong Kong-style or Cantonese barbecue, known as *siu mei* in Cantonese, is sold at many eateries in Hong Kong, from dedicated siu mei establishments, local cafes and food courts, to hotels and fine dining restaurants.

Siu mei stores usually offer roasted chicken, duck, goose, pork belly, *char siu* (barbecued pork) or barbecued pork ribs. The stores can be easily spotted due to the delicious roasted meats hanging in the windows.

Throughout the city, siu mei is prepared in different ways: from the traditional recipes still hand-roasted over charcoal to the modern techniques employed in Michelin-starred kitchens. If done right, siu mei is the perfect dish to pair with *juk* (congee), *mein* (wheat noodles) or *fun* (rice noodles). You can also order siu mei in a combo, like *sheung ping* (two types), *saam bo* (three types) or *sei bo* (four types, including a salted egg) with rice. And for local families, leftovers make a very convenient add-on to lunch or dinner, especially if you have visitors or if your kids have just called to say they'll be coming home for dinner.

Siu Ngo

Among all other siu mei, *siu ngo* (roast goose) is the heart of Hong Kong-style roast meats and is probably the most well-known dish in Hong Kong, thanks to the Michelin Guide. This delicacy is famous for its tender and juicy skin. If you have never eaten goose before, it's similar to duck but with a distinct flavour – when cooked by an expert it's sweet, tender and juicy, with glassy, crackling skin.

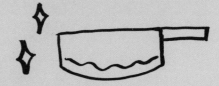

CHAR SIU

Barbecued pork

Char siu is another signature *siu mei* similar to crispy skin pork (page 70). While crispy skin pork showcases the pork belly in contrast with the crackling, char siu is famous for its sweet–savoury flavour with slightly charred skin, which instantly melts in your mouth. Delicious.

Serves 4

1 kg (2 lb 3 oz) boneless pork collar, cut lengthways into 4 pieces

fine sea salt

60 g (2 oz/½ cup) cornflour (cornstarch)

500 g (1 lb 2 oz) warmed honey

Char siu marinade

100 g (3½ oz) caster (superfine) sugar

1 tablespoon fine sea salt

2 tablespoons hoisin sauce

2 tablespoons oyster sauce

2 teaspoons sesame paste (see glossary)

1 teaspoon light soy sauce

1 teaspoon dark soy sauce

½ teaspoon finely chopped red shallot

1 teaspoon grated garlic

1 tablespoon rosé wine

1 egg, lightly beaten

Sauce

40 g (1½ oz) Chinese brown sugar (see glossary) or soft brown sugar

1 tablespoon light soy sauce

120 g (4½ oz) honey

2 teaspoons fine sea salt

1 Soak the pork in slightly salted water (about 1 teaspoon salt for every 1 litre /1 quart) for 15 minutes. Drain. Toss the pork with 40 g (1½ oz/⅓ cup) of the cornflour, then wrap in plastic wrap and marinate in the fridge for 4 hours.

2 Rinse off the cornflour and pat dry, then toss the pork in the remaining cornflour to coat well.

3 To make the marinade, mix together all the ingredients in a large bowl. Add the pork and turn to coat well, then cover and marinate in the fridge for 1 hour.

4 Preheat the oven to 240°C (465°F). Line a baking tray with foil.

5 Spread the pork out on the prepared tray and roast for 5 minutes. Turn the pork over and roast for another 5 minutes. Reduce the oven temperature to 100°C (210°F) and roast for 30 minutes. Take the pork out and turn the oven back up to 240°C (465°F).

6 Brush both sides of the pork with honey, then return to the oven and roast for 5 minutes or until the honey is bubbling and caramelising. Turn the pieces over and cook for another 5 minutes. Reduce the oven temperature to 100°C (200°F) and roast for further 30 minutes. Remove from the oven and brush with honey again.

7 Meanwhile, to make the sauce, combine all the ingredients and 3 tablespoons water in a medium saucepan. Bring to a simmer over low heat, then remove from the heat.

8 Cut the char siu into 1 cm (½ in) pieces and arrange on a serving plate. Pour the sauce over the top and serve.

BRAISED BEEF SHORT RIBS WITH DAIKON

This Cantonese-style braised beef brisket is a staple of Hong Kong restaurant menus and is a very popular dish to make at home.

What makes this stew stand out? The chu hau paste is the soul of this dish, bringing a deep richness to the beef. The daikon soaks up all the flavours and the saucy braise works perfectly with a bowl of steamed white rice. It makes a very satisfying lunch of carbs, protein and vegetables.

This stew is delicious on its own, or you can use this braise to make classic Hong Kong beef noodles. Omit the daikon and simply cook the noodles of your choice (either thin egg noodles or flat rice noodles), then add some beef stock, along with the braised beef and some of the braising liquid. You could also braise beef offal like honeycomb tripe and beef liver.

Serves 4

2 kg (4 lb 6 oz) boneless beef short ribs (or intercostal)

2 tablespoons canola oil (or other cooking oil)

200 g (7 oz) ginger, sliced

2 bunches spring (green) onions, one bunch sliced, the other cut into batons

10 garlic cloves, roughly chopped

3 red shallots, sliced

5 coriander (cilantro) roots, scraped clean (reserve leaves for garnish)

3 tablespoons chu hau paste (see Note)

2 tablespoons fermented red bean curd

125 ml (4 fl oz/½ cup) shaoxing rice wine

80 g (2¾ oz) yellow rock sugar

1 tablespoon light soy sauce

1–2 tablespoons oyster sauce

1 daikon, cut into 5 cm (2 in) pieces

1 teaspoon dark soy sauce

10 spring (green) onions, cut into 4 cm (1½ in) batons

Spice bag

3 cassia bark sticks

5 star anise

2 black cardamom pods

2 whole cloves

2 bay leaves

1 teaspoon Sichuan peppercorns

1 teaspoon coriander seeds

1 teaspoon fennel seeds

Note

Chu hau paste is a flavoursome condiment made primarily of ground fermented soy bean, mixed with sesame paste, fermented beancurd, garlic, shallot, aged mandarin peel, cinnamon and sugar. Often used in braises as it goes especially well with beef.

1 Cut the beef short ribs into 4 cm (1½ in) pieces. Soak in a bowl of water for about 10 minutes, then drain and rinse well.

2 Meanwhile, make the spice bag by putting all the spices in a small piece of muslin (cheesecloth) and fold or tie to seal. Set aside.

3 Pour 3 litres (3 quarts) water into a large saucepan or wok and add the beef. Bring to the boil and blanch for 15 minutes, then drain and rinse under cold running water to cool down. Drain and set aside to dry.

4 Wipe out the saucepan or wok, add the oil and heat over medium heat. Add the ginger, then reduce the heat to medium–low and saute for about 3 minutes. Add the sliced spring onion and the garlic, shallot and coriander root and saute for another 3 minutes or until fragrant and slightly softened.

5 Stir in the chu hau sauce, fermented red beancurd and cook over low heat for another 2 minutes. Pour in the shaoxing wine and mix well.

6 Add the beef ribs and stir to coat well with the sauce, then add the rock sugar and stir-fry for another 2 minutes. Pour in enough hot water to just cover the beef, then add the light soy sauce, 1 tablespoon of the oyster sauce and the spices bag. Cover with a lid and gently braise for 1½ hours.

7 Remove the lid – the liquid should have reduced by about half. If it still looks a bit watery, increase the heat slightly and cook, uncovered, for another 10–15 minutes. Add the daikon and mix well, then cover and braise for another 20 minutes. Remove from the heat and set aside, covered, for 20 minutes.

8 Give the beef braise a good stir, then return to low heat and braise, covered, for another 20 minutes. Keep an eye on the braising liquid – you don't want it to dry out otherwise the bottom of the beef ribs will start to burn. Add a splash of water if necessary.

9 Stir in the dark soy sauce, then taste and add another tablespoon of oyster sauce if you think it needs it. Continue to simmer, uncovered, until the sauce reaches your preferred consistency. Remove the spice bag and stir in the spring onion batons. Garnish with coriander and serve.

DOU FU FO LAM

Braised pork with tofu

Consisting of pan-fried tofu and braised roast pork belly, this dish is colloquially known as 'lonely man's favourite' as men tend to eat it alone. This is mainly because it is a dish for meat lovers and, in Hong Kong, the fatty goodness of the pork is considered to be more appealing to men than women (who are traditionally more conscious of their diets).

Serves 4

3 dried shiitake mushrooms

1 tablespoon light soy sauce

1 teaspoon canola oil (or other cooking oil)

400 g (14 oz) roasted pork belly, cut into 4 cm (1½ in) cubes

10 garlic cloves, peeled and left whole

6 red shallots, halved

6 spring (green) onions, white part only, cut into 1 cm (½ in) pieces (reserve the green parts for garnish)

6 slices ginger

200 g (7 oz) winter melon, cut into 5 cm (2 in) cubes

2 tablespoons shaoxing rice wine

8 pieces fried tofu

1 teaspoon cornflour (cornstarch)

Seasoning

1 tablespoon caster (superfine) sugar

¼ teaspoon fine sea salt

¼ teaspoon ground white pepper

1 tablespoon oyster sauce

1 teaspoon dark soy sauce

1 Soak the dried shiitake in 500 ml (17 fl oz/2 cups) tepid water for 6 hours or overnight. Remove the shiitake and reserve the soaking water. Strain it through a fine sieve to remove any dirt or sand.

2 Combine the rehydrated shiitake, soaking liquid and light soy sauce in a medium saucepan. Bring to the boil, then reduce the heat and simmer for 30 minutes. Take out the shiitake and cut each one into four thick slices. Reserve the shiitake cooking liquid.

3 Heat a large wok over high heat, add the oil, then reduce the heat to medium. Add the pork belly and stir-fry for 1 minute, then push it to one side. On the other side of the wok, add the garlic, shallot and spring onion and stir-fry until nicely golden, then add the ginger. Push all the ingredients to the side, add the shiitake and let it brown a little, then add the winter melon and toss well.

4 Pour in the shaoxing wine, followed by the reserved shiitake cooking liquid, then add the seasoning ingredients and mix well. Toss through the tofu, then reduce the heat to low, cover with a lid and braise for 7 minutes.

5 Remove the lid and give the mixture a stir. Check the level of liquid. The winter melon should have released enough moisture to stop the ingredients catching on the bottom of the wok; if not, add a splash of water and make sure the heat is as low as you can get it.

6 Put the lid back on and braise for another 7 minutes. Check the seasoning and adjust if needed.

7 Increase the heat to high and let the sauce reduce slightly. Blend the cornflour with 3 tablespoons water. Slowly pour the slurry into the wok with one hand while stirring with the other. You may not need all the slurry – just add enough to thicken the sauce to your liking.

8 Serve immediately, garnished with the sliced green part of the spring onion.

YEUNG CHAU CHOW FAN

Fried rice with barbecue pork and prawns

This fried rice dish is a great way to use up left-over prawns (shrimp), char siu and vegetables. It's easy, delicious and full of nutrients! That said, you can add anything that you want; other variants include *san chow ngau fan* (beef fried rice) and *sai chau fan* (Hong Kong-style Western fried rice with sausage and sweet-savory sauce). This makes a small serve, but you can easily increase the quantities if you have more people to feed.

Serves 2–3

Fried rice (page 179)

1 tablespoon canola oil (or other cooking oil)

100 g (3½ oz) small prawns (shrimp), peeled and deveined

100 g (3½ oz) choy sum stem, sliced

100 g (3½ oz) Char siu (page 75)

1 Prepare the fried rice to the point where the rice is flat against the wok and the moisture has started to evaporate (before you've added the seasoning and spring onion).

2 Heat the oil in a second wok over high heat, add the prawns and choy sum and stir-fry for 1 minute.

3 Add the prawns, choy sum and char siu to the rice and stir-fry for 1 minute. Now finish the fried rice with the seasoning and spring onion. Serve immediately.

STEAK WITH PEPPER SAUCE

British-influenced steakhouses became popular in Hong Kong in the 1970s. It's an entertaining bit of theatre to watch the servers at these old-school restaurants carrying three (sometimes up to five) sizzling-hot plates on one arm. Each dish is served with either a beef jus or a pepper sauce, and diners are asked to hold their paper napkin up to prevent sauce from splashing onto their clothes when the server pours it over the hot steaks. The sights, sounds and smells all contribute to a major wow factor when dining at one of these local steakhouses – another culinary example of East-meets-West in Hong Kong!

Serves 4

4 x 250 g (9 oz) beef sirloin or rib eye steaks

Pepper sauce

3 tablespoons canola oil (or other cooking oil)

8 red shallots, thinly sliced

5 long red chillies, deseeded and finely sliced

2 tablespoons finely chopped garlic

125 ml (4 fl oz/½ cup) shaoxing rice wine or red wine

3 tablespoons kecap manis

100 ml (3½ fl oz) light soy sauce

1 tablespoon freshly ground black pepper

1 tablespoon ground white pepper

1 To make the pepper sauce, heat the oil in a medium saucepan over medium heat, add the shallot and saute for 2–3 minutes until slightly softened. Add the chilli and garlic and cook for another 10 minutes.

2 Increase the heat to high and pour in the wine. Let it boil until the liquid has almost completely evaporated, then remove the pan from the heat. Add the kecap manis and soy sauce, black and white pepper, then stir well. Add 200 ml (7 fl oz) water, place over low heat and simmer for 5 minutes or until the sauce is the consistency of a gravy. Serve straight away or store in an airtight container in the fridge for up to a week.

3 Fry or barbecue the steaks to your liking, let them rest for a few minutes, then serve with the sauce.

NOODLES

In Hong Kong or Cantonese dining, there are four staple carbohydrates, at least one of which will generally be served with a meal: congee, steamed rice, rice noodles and wheat noodles.

There's no restriction on how to serve noodles, and Hong Kong people love to eat them every which way: hot or cold, dry or in soup, stir-fried or deep-fried.

Mein

Mein (wheat noodles made with egg) are the most common type used in Hong Kong. Thin wheat noodles are best with broth (such as in a wonton noodle soup) while the thicker-style wheat noodles, are perfect for stir-fries and with heartier sauces like braised beef, or in soup or even served dry.

Fan

Fan or *fun* are rice noodles. They're made with rice flour and water and usually have a soft texture and mild flavour.

Ho fan (flat rice noodles) are often used for stir-fries like *gong chow ngau ho* (fried beef noodles). You can serve them in soup – just be careful with the timing as they can overcook quite easily.

Mai fun (rice vermicelli) and *fun see* (cellophane noodles) are both very thin rice noodles that pair particularly well with seafood. Delicious in *sing chau chow mai* (Singapore noodles).

WAN TON MEIN
Wonton noodles

Wonton noodles are popular around the world but no place serves this dish like we do in Hong Kong. Freshly made wontons with a delicious prawn (shrimp) filling are served in a rich savoury broth with springy noodles and yellow chives. This dish can also be served 'dry' (*wan ton lo mein*), meaning the wontons are served on top of the noodles with no broth.

Serves 4

20 x 7 cm (2¾ in) square yellow wonton wrappers

600 g (1 lb 5 oz) wonton noodles

2 teaspoons sesame oil

1 bunch Chinese yellow chives, cut into 4 cm (1½ in) lengths

Stock

100 g (3½ oz) dried flounder (see Notes)

300 g (10½ oz) pork bone (from your local Asian butcher)

1 tablespoon sea salt

10 g (¼ oz) yellow rock sugar

2½ teaspoons dried shrimp roe (see Notes)

1 teaspoon crushed white peppercorns

60 g (2 oz) Jinhua ham (see glossary)

Wonton filling

300 g (10½ oz) prawns (shrimp), peeled and deveined

½ teaspoon fine sea salt

¼ teaspoon dried shrimp roe

¼ teaspoon dried flounder powder (see Notes)

½ teaspoon sesame powder

½ egg yolk

½ teaspoon caster (superfine) sugar

⅛ teaspoon ground white pepper

1 To make the stock, preheat the oven to 160°C (320°F). Place the dried flounder on a small baking tray and roast for 10 minutes.

2 Meanwhile, soak the pork bone in water for about 20 minutes to remove any excess blood, then give it a good rinse. Bring a medium saucepan of water to the boil, add the pork bone and blanch for about 5 minutes to remove any unpleasant smell. Drain.

3 Pour 2 litres (2 quarts) fresh water into a medium saucepan, add the pork bone and all the stock remaining ingredients and bring to a simmer, skimming off any impurities on the surface. Cover with a lid, reduce the heat to very low and simmer the stock for about 5 hours. Taste and adjust the seasoning if necessary.

4 For the wonton filling, place the prawn meat in a medium bowl and add the salt. Using a clean hand, mix in one direction for about 1 minute until the mixture starts to get sticky. Add the remaining ingredients and mix again for another 1 minute.

5 Put about 2 teaspoons of filling into each wonton wrapper, moisten the edges with water and press firmly to close.

6 Bring a large saucepan of water to the boil, carefully add the wontons and boil for about 2 minutes until tender. Remove with a slotted spoon.

7 Using the same water, blanch the wonton noodles for about 30 seconds. Remove with a flat sieve or strainer and rinse under running water to cool down, then blanch again for about 30 seconds or until just cooked.

8 Put ½ teaspoon of the sesame oil into each serving bowl and top with yellow chive batons and five wontons. Add the cooked noodles and ladle over the stock. Serve immediately.

Notes

If you can't get dried flounder, you could substitute with dried haddock from a Korean grocery. The powder is usually easier to find (substitute another dried fish powder or flake, like bonito, if unavailable) but don't use powder in the stock as it will make the soup cloudy.

Dried shrimp roe is a condiment made by curing prawn (shrimp) eggs. Look for dried shrimp roe in your Asian supermarket. The good-quality stuff can be a little expensive, but it's delicious sprinkled on anything you want to impart a salty–umami flavour to, such as tofu.

BAKED BARBECUE PORK BAO

This bun (pictured on page 90) was created by the famous Tim Ho Wan, a local Michelin-starred dim sum restaurant in Hong Kong where people line up for hours to enjoy high-quality dim sum at a humble price. This baked version marries two local favourites – barbecue pork and pineapple bun – in one delicious mouthful with a sweet, crunchy topping. Such an unusual combination now seems like a no-brainer!

Makes 12

1 tablespoon canola oil (or other cooking oil)

½ onion, finely diced

100 g (3½ oz) Char siu (page 75), finely chopped

2 tablespoons shaoxing rice wine

150 ml (5 fl oz) char siu sauce (see glossary)

Dough

170 g (6 oz) bread flour

30 g (1 oz) low-gluten flour, such as cake flour

1 teaspoon instant dry yeast

¼ teaspoon fine sea salt

2 tablespoons caster (superfine) sugar

35 g (1¼ oz) beaten egg (about ½ large egg)

30 g (1 oz) butter, softened

Shortcrust topping

60 g (2 oz) butter, softened

3 tablespoons icing (confectioners') sugar

1 small egg, beaten

60 g (2 oz) low-gluten flour, such as cake flour

small pinch of fine sea salt

1 Heat the oil in a medium saucepan over low heat, add the onion and saute for 5 minutes or until slightly softened. Add the char siu and saute for another 5 minutes, then pour in the shaoxing wine, char siu sauce and 100 ml (3½ fl oz) water. Bring to a simmer, then cook gently for about 20 minutes or until the water has almost evaporated and the char siu is soft. Set aside to cool.

2 Meanwhile, prepare the dough. Put the flour, yeast, salt, sugar, egg and 80 ml (2½ fl oz/⅓ cup) water in the bowl of a stand mixer fitted with a dough hook and mix on low speed for 15 minutes or until the dough comes together. Cover and rest for 10 minutes. Start the mixer again on medium speed, add the butter and start to mix. At first it will look sticky but this is okay. Continue to mix for 5–8 minutes or until the dough is smooth and well combined and the mixer bowl is quite clean.

3 Take a small piece of dough and do the 'windowpane' test: if you can stretch it relatively thinly without tearing it, that means the gluten has developed enough. If it tears, knead it for a bit longer and try again.

4 Transfer the dough to a medium bowl, cover with a clean damp cloth and leave the dough to prove for 1–1½ hours or until it has doubled in size. The proving time will depend on the temperature in the room – the warmer it is, the less time it will need.

5 While the dough is proving, make a start on the shortcrust topping. Combine the butter and icing sugar in a bowl, add the egg and mix until smooth. Sift in the flour and salt and mix well with a spatula. Transfer to a piping bag – no nozzle required.

6 Gently knock back the dough, then roll it into a cylinder. Cut into 12 even pieces and roll into balls. Let them rest for 15 minutes.

7 Flatten each ball of dough into an 8 cm (3¼ in) round and put about 1 tablespoon of the char siu filling in the middle. Fold over to enclose, slightly pulling and turning the dough as you go. Place on a lined tray or in a greased muffin tin, seam side down, and rest for another 20 minutes.

8 Preheat the oven to 180°C (350°F).

9 Pipe the topping onto the proved dough in a circular motion, starting in the centre and working your way out to the edge. Bake for 10–15 minutes or until golden. Remove and rest for 3 minutes, then serve hot.

LAU SA LAI WONG BAO

Runny salted egg yolk bao

If you like a molten chocolate cake, or a soft-boiled egg with runny yolk, you will understand why this runny egg-yolk custard bun is so beloved by Hongkongers. It is basically a twist on a popular dim sum creamy custard bun (*lai wong bao*), but with a lava-like salted egg-yolk filling. Be careful not to burn yourself when you bite into it!

Makes 12

3 salted duck egg yolks

1 hen's egg yolk

2 tablespoons milk powder

2 teaspoons custard powder

3 tablespoons caster (superfine) sugar

30 g (1 oz) butter, softened

Dough

250 g (9 oz/2⅔ cups) plain (all-purpose) flour

1 teaspoon instant dry yeast

1 teaspoon baking powder

1 tablespoon caster (superfine) sugar

1 Pour water into a medium saucepan to a depth of about 3 cm (1¼ in) and bring to the boil. Arrange all the egg yolks on a steamer tray or plate, then cover and steam for 10 minutes or until fully cooked.

2 Transfer to a small bowl and mash with a fork. Mix in the powders, sugar and butter until well combined, then cover and put in the fridge for 15 minutes.

3 To make the dough, place the flour, yeast, baking powder and sugar in a large bowl and mix well. Add 125 ml (4 fl oz/½ cup) water and stir gently with your hand until all the ingredients start to come together. Gently knead the dough in the bowl for 5 minutes, then cover with plastic wrap and leave to rest for 10 minutes.

4 Turn out the dough onto a clean bench and knead for another 10 minutes or until smooth.

5 Put the dough in a medium bowl, cover with a clean damp cloth and leave the dough to prove for 1–1½ hours or until it has nearly doubled in size.

6 Meanwhile, turn the egg filling out and portion into 12 even-sized balls. Cover with plastic wrap and return to the fridge.

7 Gently knock back the dough, then roll it into a cylinder. Cut into 12 even pieces and roll into balls. Let them rest for 5 minutes.

8 Flatten each ball of dough into an 8 cm (3¼ in) round with thinner edges and put a portion of egg filling in the middle. Fold over to enclose, slightly pulling and turning the dough as you go. Place on a lined tray, seam side down, and rest for another 15 minutes.

9 Pour water into a large saucepan to a depth of about 3 cm (1¼ in) and bring to the boil. Arrange the buns on a steamer tray or plate in a single layer, then cover and steam for 10 minutes. Depending on the size of your steamer you may need to do this in two batches.

10 Serve immediately, and be careful as the egg filling will be like hot running lava!

Left: Runny salted egg yolk bao;
right: Baked barbecue pork bao, page 88

HUNG DAO PING

Red bean crushed ice drink

A favourite among kids since the 1970s, this sweet, icy cold drink is a stunning series of layers and textures: the vivid red colour of the beans and the crisp white of the coconut milk, often topped with vanilla ice cream. A drink and dessert in one, this is wonderfully refreshing on a hot day.

Serves 4

100 g (3½ oz) dried red (adzuki) beans (see Note)

300 g (10½ oz) yellow rock sugar

3 large handfuls crushed ice

200 ml (7 fl oz) coconut milk

200 ml (7 fl oz) evaporated milk

4 scoops vanilla ice cream (optional)

1 Soak the red beans in water overnight (this will significantly shorten the cooking time).

2 Drain the beans and tip into a medium saucepan. Add 400 ml (13½ fl oz) water and cook over medium heat for about 1 hour or until the beans are soft.

3 Pour in enough water to just cover the beans, then add the rock sugar and cook until the sugar has dissolved and the beans are fully cooked, with an almost sandy texture. Allow to cool, then transfer to the fridge to chill.

4 Spoon the red bean mixture into four tall glasses until they are half full, then top up with crushed ice. Divide the coconut milk and evaporated milk evenly among the glasses. Finish with a scoop of ice cream, if you like, then serve immediately with a straw and spoon, stirring well as you eat and drink.

Note

This makes more red beans than you will need here. Store leftover cooked beans in an airtight container in the fridge for up to 4 days, or in the freezer for 2 weeks. It's always worth making more than you need as preparing the beans is the most time-consuming part of the process. If you have extra on hand you can make this drink whenever you feel like in no time! Or use them in the red bean puddings on page 96.

PUT CHAI GO

Red bean puddings in little bowls

These delicious pudding are made with rice flour, red beans and brown sugar syrup (for the brown ones, which we are making here) or coconut milk (for the white ones). The method is quite simple but make sure you follow the instructions to ensure you achieve the right texture. So beloved is this pudding, some of the traditional stores will mill rice every day to get fresh rice 'milk' to make it!

Serves 4

100 g (3½ oz) good-quality dried red (adzuki) beans, rinsed (see Note)

3 tablespoons caster (superfine) sugar

80 g (2¾ oz) rice flour

2 tablespoons wheat starch

1 tablespoon cornflour (cornstarch)

100 g (3½ oz) Chinese brown sugar (see glossary) or soft brown sugar

1 Soak the beans in a bowl of water for 30 minutes. Drain and place in a small saucepan. Add 500 ml (17 fl oz/2 cups) water and bring to the boil over high heat, then reduce the heat and simmer for 45 minutes, skimming off any impurities on the surface.

2 Reduce the heat to low, add the sugar and cook, stirring regularly, for another 30 minutes or until the beans are cooked but still retain their shape. Remove from the heat, cover with a lid and set aside for 2 hours or until cooled completely.

3 Meanwhile, combine the rice flour, wheat starch and cornflour in a medium bowl, add 250 ml (8½ fl oz/1 cup) water and stir until smooth.

4 Pour 250 ml (8½ fl oz/1 cup) water into a small saucepan and bring to the boil. Add the brown sugar and stir until dissolved.

5 Pour the hot sugar syrup into the flour mixture and mix until smooth and well combined.

6 Grease four individual heatproof bowls or ramekins. Put 1 teaspoon of the red beans into each bowl (or a bit more if you like).

7 Give the sugar and flour mixture a really good stir (otherwise the flour tends to settle at the bottom), then pour into the bowls until they are about four-fifths full. Finish with another teaspoon of the beans

8 Pour water into a large saucepan to a depth of about 3 cm (1¼ in) and bring to the boil. Arrange the bowls or ramekins on a steamer tray or plate, then cover and steam for 20 minutes.

9 Remove and rest for 5 minutes, then serve hot. If you like, you can turn the puddings out of the bowls and serve on skewers like a streetside snack.

Note

If you have any beans left over from the crushed ice recipe on page 95, use them here to save time.

SHEUNG PEI LAI

'Double-skin' milk custards

Double skin milk custard is a very creamy, yet light and silky Cantonese dessert made with milk, egg whites and sugar. Similar to a panna cotta, double-skin milk dates back to the 19th century in Guangdong, China. Although it does not have a particularly appetising name (imagine a dessert with double skin!), it is full of nutrients and many Hong Kong women believe it has beautifying effects on their skin.

As with all simple recipes it's important to use the best ingredients you can find. Use top-quality full-cream milk for the best possible flavour while doubling up on your protein!

Serves 6

1 litre (1 quart/4 cups) full-cream (whole) milk

10 egg whites

160 g (5½ oz) caster (superfine) sugar

1 Pour the milk into a medium saucepan and bring to a simmer over low heat (about 80–90°C/170–190°F).

2 Pour the milk evenly into six 250 ml (8½ fl oz/1 cup) bowls and let it cool, ideally with a fan, which helps a skin form. This should take about 30 minutes.

3 Using a chopstick, lightly poke a small hole in the skin at 12 o'clock and 6 o'clock. Gently pour the milk from the 12 o'clock hole into a medium bowl, keeping the chopstick in the hole to prevent the skin from pouring off with it. Keep pouring until there is about 1 tablespoon of milk and the milk skin left in the bowl. Repeat with the other bowls. It's important to keep some milk in the bowl otherwise the milk skin will stick to the bottom of the bowl.

4 Using a fork, lightly whisk the egg whites. Try not to incorporate any air otherwise the end result won't be smooth.

5 Stir the sugar into the milk until it has completely dissolved. Mix in the egg white, then carefully strain to remove any bubbles. Gently pour the milk mixture back into the bowls from the side, until about four-fifths full. As you do this, the skin formed earlier will rise to the surface. Wrap each bowl with plastic wrap.

6 Pour water into a large saucepan or wok to a depth of about 3 cm (1¼ in) and bring to the boil. Reduce the heat slightly to medium–high. Arrange the bowls on a steamer tray or plate, then cover and steam for 5–8 minutes until starting to set. Leave the bowls in the steamer, then remove from the heat and rest, covered, for another 8–10 minutes. (Depending on the size of your steamer you may need to steam the bowls in batches.)

7 Give each bowl a gentle shake – if the milk in the centre has a slight wobble, it's ready. If it is still looking quite watery, steam for a bit longer and check again.

8 Remove the plastic wrap, allow to cool slightly for 1 minute, then serve hot.

GINGER CUSTARDS

This creamy dessert is very quick to prepare and then it's just a matter of steaming it to wobbly perfection. All you need are eggs, milk, sugar and ginger (although you can even leave the ginger out if you prefer a plain custard).

Serves 6

300 g (10½ oz) caster (superfine) sugar

1 litre (1 quart/4 cups) full-cream (whole) milk

10 cm (4 in) piece ginger, finely grated

6 eggs

1 Combine the sugar and 500 ml (17 fl oz/2 cups) of the milk in a saucepan and cook over medium heat, stirring until the sugar has dissolved.

2 Meanwhile, place the ginger in a fine strainer and press down to release the juice into the bowl. You will need about 2½ tablespoons of juice. Combine the juice with the remaining milk.

3 Lightly beat the eggs until loosened, then whisk into the cold ginger milk mixture. Add this to the warm milk and sugar mixture and whisk to combine. Pour through a sieve into six small bowls (about 150 ml/5 fl oz) and cover tightly with foil.

4 Pour water into a large saucepan or wok to a depth of about 3 cm (1¼ in) and bring to the boil. Reduce the heat to low. Arrange the bowls on a steamer tray or plate, then cover and steam for 12 minutes or until just set with a slight wobble. (Depending on the size of your steamer you may need to steam the bowls in batches.)

5 Serve the custards hot or put them in the fridge and serve chilled.

YEUNG CHI KAM LO

Sago with coconut, mango and pomelo

This refreshing mango soup was created by a Hong Kong chef in the 1980s. Served chilled, its popularity lies in just the right balance of flavours and textures – the soft, sweet mango, light coconut cream, chewy sago pearls and slightly bitter pomelo popping in the mouth. Hongkongers consider it a staple in the dessert world.

Serves 4

150 g (5½ oz) sago (tapioca) pearls

150 ml (5 fl oz) evaporated milk

3 ripe mangoes, peeled, flesh finely diced

1 pomelo

Coconut syrup

100 g (3½ oz) yellow rock sugar, or to taste

200 ml (7 fl oz) coconut cream

tiny pinch of fine sea salt

1 To make the coconut syrup, place the sugar and 1 litre (1 quart/4 cups) water in a medium saucepan and gently bring to the boil over low heat, stirring occasionally to dissolve the sugar. Remove from the heat. Add the coconut cream and salt and mix well, then set side to cool.

2 Pour 1 litre (1 quart/4 cups) water into a medium saucepan and bring to the boil. Add the sago and boil for about 8 minutes, stirring occasionally to stop it sticking to the bottom of the pan. Remove from the heat, then cover with a lid and set aside for 15–20 minutes until the sago is just cooked and transparent.

3 Drain and rinse the sago under cold running water to cool it to room temperature, then add it to the cooled coconut syrup.

4 Blend the evaporated milk and two-thirds of the mango until smooth, then add to the sago mixture and mix well. Scoop it into a serving bowl, then cover and chill in the fridge for 1 hour.

5 Peel the pomelo, then gently separate the flesh into small pieces. Add to the sago mixture, along with the remaining mango, and serve cold.

SMILEY COOKIES

These deep-fried sesame balls are especially popular during Chinese New Year. The name comes from the cracks that develop after deep-frying, which resemble a smiling face on each cookie.

The key here is to control the oil temperature. Start off low to gently cook the dough until it rises to the surface, then cook the cookies a second time in hotter oil to give them a crisp, short finish.

Makes about 30

80 g (2¾ oz/⅓ cup) caster (superfine) sugar

1 teaspoon baking powder

¼ teaspoon baking soda

¼ teaspoon fine sea salt

1 egg, lightly beaten

40 g (1½ oz) lard or butter, softened

200 g (7 oz/1⅓ cups) cake flour

iced water, for dipping

100 g (3½ oz) white sesame seeds

2 litres (2 quarts) canola oil (or other cooking oil)

1 Place the sugar, baking powder, baking soda, salt and 2 tablespoons water in a medium bowl and mix until the sugar has dissolved. Add the egg and mix well, then stir in the lard or butter.

2 Add the flour and gently mix to form a soft dough. (Don't overwork the dough as this will develop the gluten and make the biscuits tough). Cover with plastic wrap and leave to rest for 30 minutes.

3 On a lightly floured surface, roll the dough into a long cylinder and cut into 30 even pieces. Roll each piece into a ball, then gently flatten into a round, fold over, and roughly shape into a ball again (you want the ball to have a bit of a crack left in it from where you folded it, as this is what opens out into the 'smile' when it's cooked).

4 Prepare a bowl of iced water, and pour the sesame seeds into another bowl.

5 Quickly dip the balls into the iced water, then roll them in the sesame seeds until evenly coated.

6 Pour the oil into a medium saucepan and heat over medium heat to 160°C (320°F) or until a cube of bread dropped in the oil browns in 30–35 seconds. Add a few sesame balls at a time so you don't overcrowd the pan. Keep them moving and turning in the oil for 4–6 minutes or until golden brown all over. Remove with a slotted spoon.

7 When you've finished, strain the oil into another clean saucepan to remove the sesame seeds. Increase the heat to high and heat the oil to 180°C (350°F) or until a cube of bread dropped in the oil browns in 15 seconds. Working in batches again, fry the sesame balls for 1 minute to achieve a crisp and crunchy texture. Remove with a slotted spoon and drain on paper towel. These are best served warm but you could let them cool and store them in an airtight container for up to 2 days.

Late

While lunch for many in Hong Kong is usually a quick, convenient and solo affair, dinner is all about getting together with family and friends. If you've never experienced it, you absolutely have to try hotpot when you're in Hong Kong – and there are plenty of options! Even if you've had hotpot before, nothing compares to Hong Kong hotpot. You select all kinds of ingredients in raw form – from fish balls, mushrooms and vegetables, to wagyu beef slices, prawns and premium seafood – then you can choose your soup base (or a few – why stop at one?), with everything from pork bone soup, satay, mala and tomato, to chicken and fish maw, deluxe mushroom – the choices are endless. It's the perfect way to dine with friends.

Hong Kong is heaven for seafood lovers, and, especially if you venture to areas like Lei Yue Mun, Sai Kung, Tuen Mun and Lamma Island, you'll find countless restaurants that specialise in live seafood. You can choose the seafood you want and the restaurant will cook it for you in the style that you like: such as steamed scallops with glass noodles, stir-fried clams or razor clams with black bean and chilli, typhoon shelter crab, cheesy lobster with noodles ... and you have to try *ching yu* (steamed whole fish with soy and spring onion), a staple Cantonese dish that we Hong Kongers are very proud of.

Don't just settle for three meals in a day. In Hong Kong, late-night supper is known as *siu yeh*, and it's a true fourth meal that's an essential way to unwind for locals after a very long work day (and a godsend for tourists who need somethig to soak up a bellyful of cocktails). Try an oyster omelette or masterstock duck at a Chiu Chow *daa laang* restaurant, or a bowl of *san gwan* congee from a *dai pai dong*.

Hongkongers love sweet things at all times of the day, but at night the offerings are especially plentiful. If you like chewy, look for glutinous rice balls, taro balls or tapioca; if you like fruity you'll find mango or mixed melon in coconut milk; if you like crunchy and cold there's shaved ice with red bean and condensed milk; if you like hot and healthy get yourself some steamed white fungus with dates in coconut.

As a food paradise, Hong Kong has everything covered.

HOT POT

CHIU CHOW OYSTER OMELETTE

Unlike most of the West, in Chiu Chow cuisine, oysters are cooked. This pan-fried omelette is a great example, featuring baby oysters and duck eggs in the batter. If you can't get hold of fresh duck eggs use three hen's eggs instead, and if baby oysters are unavailable, small oysters (about 3 cm/1¼ in) will work just as well.

Serves 2

2 duck eggs

1 tablespoon sweet potato flour

2 tablespoons chopped spring (green) onion

½ teaspoon fine sea salt

¼ teaspoon ground white pepper

½ teaspoon sesame oil

80 ml (2½ fl oz/⅓ cup) canola oil (or other cooking oil)

coriander (cilantro) leaves, to serve

Oysters

150 g (5½ oz) shucked baby oysters (10–15 oysters)

1 teaspoon cornflour (cornstarch)

1 teaspoon canola oil (or other cooking oil)

1 To prepare the oysters, mix together the oysters, cornflour and oil. Gently massage so the liquid from the oysters sticks to the cornflour.

2 Bring a medium saucepan of water to the boil. Blanch the oysters for 10 seconds, then remove and drain on paper towel.

3 Lightly beat the eggs and sweet potato flour, then add the blanched oysters, spring onion, salt and pepper and sesame oil.

4 Heat a medium non-stick frying pan over high heat. When the pan is hot, add the canola oil and swirl to coat the base. Add the oyster and egg mixture, give it a quick mix as if you were making scrambled egg, then stop mixing so you get a nice colour on the egg. Cook for about 2 minutes, then flip the omelette over and cook for another 2 minutes or until golden brown on both sides.

5 Transfer to a plate, sprinkle with chopped coriander and serve immediately.

SAN GWAN JUK

Quick congee

This Hong Kong-style congee differs from other congees in both the way it is cooked (a method called *san gwan*) and the versatility of ingredients (similar to fried rice). The ingredients are usually stir-fried over high heat to release the initial fragrance, then finish cooking in a slightly loose congee. This way all the flavours and juices are absorbed into the congee, and the fish or meat is less likely to dry out because of the quick cooking process. A step up from a humble breakfast congee, this one is fresh and flavourful, but still comforting.

Serves 4

200 g (7 oz) white fish fillet, such as cod, whiting or barramundi, patted dry and thickly sliced

½ teaspoon ground white pepper

1 tablespoon light soy sauce

1 tablespoon cornflour (cornstarch)

500 ml (17 fl oz/2 cups) Basic congee (page 13)

125 ml (4 fl oz/½ cup) chicken stock or water

1 tablespoon canola oil (or other cooking oil)

1 teaspoon thinly sliced ginger

1 tablespoon shaoxing rice wine

thinly sliced spring (green) onion, to serve

coriander (cilantro) leaves, to serve

1 Place the fish, white pepper, soy sauce and cornflour in a medium bowl and toss together well. Cover and leave to marinate in the fridge for 30 minutes.

2 Warm up the congee and stock or water in a medium saucepan over medium heat.

3 Meanwhile, heat the oil in a medium saucepan (preferably non-stick) over high heat, add the ginger and fish in a single layer. Leave the fish untouched for about 30 seconds, then add the shaoxing wine. Pour in the congee mixture and bring to the boil to cook the fish. This should take about 10 minutes.

4 Ladle into bowls, garnish with the spring onion and coriander and serve immediately.

STEAMED WHOLE FISH WITH SOY AND SPRING ONION

Steamed whole fish is a classic dish in Hong Kong. It's one of the best ways to eat fish and needs only a few condiments. This cooking method emphasises the freshness of the seafood and preserves the natural flavours of all the ingredients. The fish is steamed until it is just cooked at the bone and served in a slightly sweetened soy sauce with plenty of spring onion and ginger, then doused with super-hot oil for the fragrance. Serve with freshly steamed rice – I can easily finish two bowls of rice with just the sauce!

Serves 4

140 ml (4½ fl oz) canola oil (or other cooking oil)

1 bunch (about 200 g/7 oz) spring (green) onions, ½ bunch cut into 7.5 cm (3 in) batons, white parts of the remainder sliced into rounds and green parts julienned

4 cm (1½ in) piece ginger, sliced

2 tablespoons roughly chopped red shallot

1 tablespoon roughly chopped coriander (cilantro) root

2 tablespoons shaoxing rice wine

1 tablespoon caster (superfine) sugar

100 ml (3½ fl oz) light soy sauce

1 tablespoon oyster sauce

1 x 1.2 kg (2 lb 10 oz) grouper, gutted, cleaned and scaled

1 Heat 2 tablespoons of the oil in a wok or frying pan over medium heat, add the sliced spring onion whites and the ginger, shallot and coriander root and saute for about 1 minute or until fragrant. Add the shaoxing wine, sugar and 100 ml (3½ fl oz) water. Bring to the boil, then reduce the heat and simmer for 30 seconds. Remove from the heat and stir in the soy sauce and oyster sauce.

2 Pour water into a large wok or frying pan to a depth of about 3 cm (1¼ in) and bring to the boil.

3 If you can, find a steamer tray or heatproof plate that is slightly larger than the fish. (If not, you can cut the fish into six pieces. If you do this, the fish will cook more quickly – start checking from about 8 minutes.)

4 Place the spring onion batons on the tray or plate and put the fish on top. (The spring onion keeps the fish from touching the tray or plate, ensuring the fish cooks evenly.) Put the plate in the wok or pan, cover with a lid and steam for 12 minutes. Turn the heat off and leave, covered, for another minute.

5 Insert a chopstick into the thickest part of the fish – if it goes in easily without too much force, the fish is cooked. Remove the plate or tray from the steamer and scatter the julienned spring onion over the fish.

6 Heat the remaining 100 ml (3½ fl oz) of oil in a small saucepan over high heat until it is smoking hot, then carefully pour the hot oil over the spring onion. Pour the sweetened soy sauce over the fish and serve immediately.

STEAMED SCALLOPS WITH GLASS NOODLES

This is simply the best way to eat scallops or razor clams, and is usually served as a starter. Bringing the clean fresh flavours of the ocean to the table, the scallops are flavoured with fried garlic and soy, and the noodles soak up all the delicious juices.

Serves 4

2 tablespoons light soy sauce

1 teaspoon caster (superfine) sugar

1 tablespoon minced garlic

1 tablespoon fried garlic
(see page 120)

20 g (¾ oz) glass noodles, soaked and drained

8 fresh scallops on the half shell, rinsed

2 tablespoons thinly sliced spring (green) onion, green part only

1 Place the soy sauce, sugar and 2 tablespoons of water in a small bowl and mix until the sugar has dissolved. Stir in the minced garlic and fried garlic.

2 Cut the noodles into 5 cm (2 in) lengths. Place a thin layer of noodles onto the scallop shells, underneath the scallops. Spoon the garlic and soy sauce over the top.

3 Pour water into a large saucepan to a depth of about 3 cm (1¼ in) and bring to the boil.

4 Arrange the scallop shells on a steamer tray or plate (without overlapping), then cover and steam for 1½–2 minutes or until the scallops are just cooked. Depending on the size of your steamer you may need to do this in two batches. Sprinkle with spring onion and serve hot.

BLACK BEAN CHILLI CLAMS

We all know about the famous XO pipis, but this is a great way to enjoy the taste of Hong Kong seafood. The clams are more than equal to the strong flavours of the salted black beans and chilli – it's no wonder this is such a popular dish.

Serves 2 (but if you really like clams, it's all yours)

1 kg (2 lb 3 oz) fresh clams or pipis, purged

125 ml (4 fl oz/½ cup) shaoxing rice wine

2 tablespoons canola oil (or other cooking oil)

2 tablespoons finely chopped garlic

1 tablespoon salted black beans, finely chopped

2 red bird's eye chillies, deseeded and chopped

1 tablespoon oyster sauce

125 ml (4 fl oz/½ cup) chicken stock

1 teaspoon cornflour (cornstarch), blended with 2 tablespoons water

3–4 spring (green) onions, finely sliced

1 Heat a large frying pan over high heat until it is really hot. Add the clams and wine, then cover with a lid and cook for 1 minute. Take out the clams as they start to open, then strain and reserve the clam juice. Discard any clams that don't open.

2 Taste the clam juice: if it is quite salty only use about 2 tablespoons in the next step, otherwise you can use more to suit your taste.

3 Heat the oil in a large clean frying pan over high heat, add the garlic and salted black bean and saute for 30 seconds. Add the chilli and saute for another 30 seconds, then add the clams and stir well. Pour in the oyster sauce, chicken stock and reserved clam juice and bring to simmer. Gradually stir in enough of the cornflour slurry until to thicken the sauce to your preferred consistency (you may not need it all).

4 Serve immediately, topped with spring onion.

CHEESY LOBSTER

For Hong Kong locals there is nothing strange abut the combination of cheese and lobster. The flavour and texture of live lobster goes hand-in-hand with the cheese sauce, and the *yi mein* (egg noodles that represent long life or longevity) underneath absorb the creamy sauce, making them extra delicious. This will definitely satisfy your cheese craving!

If you're confident to buy live lobster, choose ones that are heavy, active and not too sleepy, with no bubbling around the mouth or damage on the shell or claws.

Serves 4

2 lobsters

iced water, to refresh

2 tablespoons cornflour (cornstarch)

1 litre (1 quart/4 cups) canola oil (or other cooking oil)

250 g (9 oz) yi mein noodles (or other flat egg noodles)

40 g (1½ oz) butter

2 tablespoons finely chopped garlic

1 tablespoon sliced ginger

4 red shallots, thinly sliced

6 slices cheddar cheese

500 ml (17 fl oz/2 cups) chicken stock

1 teaspoon caster (superfine) sugar

2 tablespoons thinly sliced spring (green) onion

1 Bring 5 litres (5 quarts) water to the boil in a large saucepan, add the lobsters and blanch for 1 minute (if your lobsters are live, plunging them into boiling water will kill them instantly). Remove and refresh in iced water.

2 Using a cleaver, cut each lobster in half lengthways, and then in half again widthways. Remove the gills. Strain off any excess liquid, then pat the lobster dry and lightly coat with cornflour.

3 Pour the oil into a large wok and heat to about 170°C (340°F) or until a cube of bread dropped in the oil browns in 20 seconds. Add the lobster pieces and fry for about 2 minutes or until nearly cooked. Remove the lobster with a slotted spoon. Strain the oil and reserve for another use.

4 Bring 1 litre (1 quart/4 cups) water to the boil in a medium saucepan, add the noodles and cook for 1–2 minutes or until loosened. Drain and cool under cold running water.

5 Melt the butter in a large wok or frying pan over medium heat, add the garlic, ginger and shallot and saute for 1 minute or until softened. Add the cheese, chicken stock and sugar and bring to a simmer, stirring until the cheese has melted and the sauce is smooth and well combined.

6 Add the lobster and cook for 3 minutes, then add the noodles and cook for 1 minute. The sauce should be thick enough to coat the noodles – if it's still quite runny, dish up the noodles and lobster first, then simmer the sauce until it has thickened to your liking.

7 Plate the noodles, then the lobster pieces, and pour the cheese sauce over the top. Sprinkle with spring onion and serve.

TYPHOON SHELTER CRAB

The typhoon shelter crab is one of the most iconic and must-try seafood dishes in Hong Kong. Originating from the shelters for fishing boats during typhoon seasons, this dish is known for its strong flavours of chilli and garlic. Spicy and crunchy, it's a dish that will keep you going back for more!

Serves 4

1 whole mud crab (about 1 kg/ 2 lb 3 oz)

iced water, for soaking

125 ml (4 fl oz/½ cup) light soy sauce

250 ml (8½ fl oz/1 cup) shaoxing rice wine

250 g (9 oz/2 cups) cornflour (cornstarch)

2 red shallots, finely chopped

2 tablespoons salted black beans, rinsed and chopped

2 red bird's eye chillies, chopped

fine sea salt

2 spring (green) onions, chopped

Fried garlic

20 garlic cloves, finely chopped

2 litres (2 quarts) canola oil (or other cooking oil)

4 cm (1½ in) piece ginger, sliced

3 dried bird's eye chillies

pinch of fine sea salt

1 To make the fried garlic, rinse the garlic in water for 2 minutes, drain well and spread out on paper towel to dry for 15 minutes.

2 Pour the oil into a wok or large frying pan and heat to 160°C (320°F) or until a cube of bread dropped in the oil browns in 30–35 seconds. Add the ginger, then the garlic and reduce the heat to medium. Cook, stirring gently, for 30 seconds, then add the dried chilli, stirring so it doesn't all clump together. Cook until the garlic is lightly golden, then strain into a clean saucepan (reserve the oil for cooking the crab). Spread out the garlic mixture on paper towel to drain and cool. As it cools it will become crispy. Season with salt, then store in an airtight container. It will keep for up to 4 days.

3 Place the crab on a board with the belly side facing up. Pull away the triangular shell and give the crab a good rinse under running water. Remove the claws and rinse. Pry the top shell away from the body, then get rid of the gills. Remove the head and eyes. Cut the crab in half, then in half again between the legs to make four even pieces. Remove the large and small claws with the back of a cleaver or knife. Wrap the claws in a tea towel and crack them with the flat side of the cleaver or a knife.

4 Combine the soy sauce and 125 ml (4 fl oz/½ cup) shaoxing wine in a glass or ceramic dish. Add the crab and coat in the mixture, then leave to marinate for 15 minutes. Remove and dust the crab pieces in cornflour (this will prevent it from overcooking in the hot oil).

5 Pour the reserved garlic oil into a large wok or saucepan and heat to 160°C (320°F) or until a cube of bread dropped in the oil browns in 30–35 seconds. Reduce the heat to medium, add the large claw first and cook for 1 minute. Add the smaller claws and cook for 30 seconds, then add the leg pieces and cook for another 30 seconds. Add the shell, meat side up, and gently scoop some of the hot oil into the shell to cook the meat. This should take about 30 seconds. Remove the crab pieces with a slotted spoon, and strain and reserve the oil.

6 Pour 125 ml (4 fl oz/½ cup) of the reserved oil into a wok or saucepan and heat over medium heat. Add the shallot, black bean and chilli and cook for 1 minute or until slightly caramelised. Add the crab and a pinch or two of salt and gently toss to combine and coat.

7 Add the remaining shaoxing wine and cook, tossing, until all the liquid has evaporated (take care as the wine might catch fire!). Add the spring onion and 3 tablespoons of the fried garlic and toss to combine. Scoop into a serving dish with the shell on top, sprinkle with the remaining fried garlic and serve.

CHIU YIM SIN YAU

Salt and pepper squid

Salt and pepper squid is a crispy, salty and slightly spicy dish that also works well with prawn (shrimp) and cuttlefish, and even tofu if you don't eat seafood. You could also stir-fry some garlic and spring onion in a large frying pan, then add the deep-fried squid and stir-fry for 30 seconds for extra fragrance.

Serves 4

100 g (3½ oz) glutinous rice flour

100 g (3½ oz) rice flour

100 g (3½ oz) tapioca starch

175 ml (6 fl oz) sparkling water

1 litre (1 quart/4 cups) canola oil (or other cooking oil)

2 x 200 g (7 oz) squid hoods, cleaned, cut into 7.5 cm x 1 cm (3 in x ½ in) strips

1 teaspoon fine sea salt

1 teaspoon freshly ground black pepper

2 teaspoon ground white pepper

1 teaspoon ground green Sichuan pepper (otherwise red will do)

1 long red chilli, deseeded and sliced

2 spring (green) onions, green parts sliced

1 Mix together the glutinous rice flour, rice flour and tapioca starch, then divide evenly between two bowls.

2 Blend the sparkling water into one bowl of flour to form a smooth batter.

3 Pour the oil into a large wok or saucepan and heat to 180°C (350°F) or until a cube of bread dropped in the oil browns in 15 seconds.

4 Meanwhile, pat the squid dry, then lightly coat it in the remaining flour mixture, shaking off the excess.

5 Dip the squid into the batter, allowing any excess to drip off, then gently lower into the oil. Fry the squid for 1 minute or until cooked and lightly golden. Remove with a slotted spoon and drain on paper towel.

6 Transfer to a bowl and toss with the salt, peppers, chilli and spring onion and serve hot.

STEAMED RICE WITH PRAWN AND LOTUS LEAF

What's the best part of this dish? I would have to say the rice. It absorbs the flavour of the garlic, the prawn (shrimp) juices and the fragrance of the lotus leaf. The perfect simple yet tasty dish! Even simpler if you have chilled leftover rice from the day before.

Serves 2

200 g (7 oz/1 cup) jasmine rice

100 ml (3½ fl oz) canola oil (or other cooking oil)

2 egg whites

½ teaspoon fine sea salt

¼ teaspoon ground white pepper

8 garlic cloves, chopped

1 dried lotus leaf (see glossary)

4 fresh tiger prawns (shrimp), peeled and deveined, halved lengthways

4 spring (green) onions, white parts thinly sliced into rounds, green parts julienned

2 cm (1½ in) piece ginger, sliced

1 tablespoon roughly chopped red shallot

½ tablespoon roughly chopped coriander (cilantro) root

1 tablespoon shaoxing rice wine

½ tablespoon caster (superfine) sugar

2½ tablespoons light soy sauce

½ tablespoon oyster sauce

1 Cook the rice using a rice cooker. Set aside to cool.

2 Heat a large wok or frying pan over high heat. Add 2 tablespoons of the oil and as soon as it is hot add the egg white and stir for 5 seconds. Add the cooled rice and stir-fry until the rice is coated with the egg white. Season with salt and pepper, then transfer to a plate.

3 Wipe out the wok or frying pan, add another 2 tablespoons of the oil and heat over medium heat. Add 2 tablespoon chopped garlic and fry for 1 minute or until lightly golden. Scoop the garlic and oil into a small bowl and mix with the remaining chopped garlic.

4 Grab a large wok or frying pan with a lid that will fit a 25.5 cm (10 in) bamboo steamer basket. Add 2 litres (2 quarts) water and bring to the boil. Quickly blanch the lotus leaf so it turns soft, then remove.

5 Line the bamboo basket with the lotus leaf, then spoon in the rice and top with the eight prawn halves, meat side up. Spoon over the garlic mixture. Fold the lotus leaf over so it covers the prawns and rice. Bring the water in the wok or pan to the boil again, then steam the prawns for 10 minutes.

6 Meanwhile, heat the remaining 1 tablespoon of the oil in a small frying pan over medium heat, add the sliced spring onion whites and the ginger, shallot and coriander root and saute for about 1 minute or until fragrant. Add the shaoxing wine, sugar and 2½ tablespoons of water. Bring to the boil, then reduce the heat and simmer for 30 seconds. Remove from the heat and stir in the soy sauce and oyster sauce.

7 Open up the lotus leaf, pour over the sweetened soy sauce and garnish with the spring onion greens. Serve immediately.

PRAWN TOASTS

Looking for a crowd-pleasing party snack? Prawn toasts will be loved by friends and family of all ages. The secret weapon in this recipe is the combination of roughly and finely chopped prawns (shrimp) for extra texture.

Makes 16

4 slices white bread, crusts removed, each cut into 4 triangles

50 g (1¾ oz/⅓ cup) white sesame seeds

500 ml (17 fl oz/2 cups) canola oil (or other cooking oil)

thinly sliced spring (green) onion, to garnish

mayonnaise or tomato ketchup, to serve

Prawn mixture

200 g (7 oz) peeled, deveined prawns (shrimp)

2 tablespoons cornflour (cornstarch)

1 teaspoon fine sea salt

1 teaspoon caster (superfine) sugar

small pinch of ground white pepper

1 teaspoon grated garlic

1 teaspoon grated ginger

½ egg white

1 To make the prawn mixture, toss the prawns with 1 tablespoon cornflour, then rinse in cool water and pat dry with paper towel. Roughly chop the prawn meat, divide in half and very finely chop half of it. Place the prawn meat into a bowl, sprinkle the salt over the top and mix until the prawn mixture becomes elastic. Add the remaining ingredients and mix well.

2 Spread 2 teaspoons of the prawn mixture over each bread triangle. Make sure you spread it all the way to the edges and form a smooth, even surface. Dip the bread, prawn side down, into the sesame seeds to coat.

3 Pour the oil into a wok or a small saucepan (it should be about one-third full) and heat to 180°C (350°F) or until a cube of bread dropped in the oil browns in 15 seconds. Reduce the heat to low. Working in batches, add the toasts, prawn side down, and cook for 1 minute. Turn them over and cook for a further 15–30 seconds until the toast is golden. Remove with a slotted spoon and drain on a wire rack or paper towel. Serve hot garnished with spring onion and with mayonnaise or ketchup on the side.

MASTERSTOCK GOOSE

Goose is quite common in Hong Kong but not everywhere else so you may need to order one from your butcher. It's similar to duck but it has a unique taste, especially the fatty part with the skin. This dish is all about the sauce the goose is cooked in, and relies on having a good basic masterstock. If you're dining in Hong Kong, do not miss out on this dish – you can usually order it as part of a platter that includes things like goose slices, duck wings, tofu, pork and squid.

Serves 4

1 x 1.5–1.8 kg (3 lb 5 oz–4 lb) whole goose, any giblets removed and bird well rinsed and patted dry with paper towel

iced water, to refresh

Masterstock (page 170)

sliced spring (green) onion, to garnish

chopped coriander (cilantro) leaves, to garnish

1 Pour 5 litres (5 quarts) water into a stockpot large enough to fit the goose and bring to the boil over high heat. Add the goose and lay it flat so the hot water can go inside the body as well. Blanch for 30 seconds. Drain, then transfer the goose to a large bowl of iced water to soak for 5 minutes.

2 Bring the masterstock to the boil in the stockpot.

3 Add the goose and bring the masterstock back to the boil, then reduce the heat to low and simmer for 45 minutes. Take the pan off the heat and and let the goose cool in the stock for 1 hour.

4 Transfer the goose to a large plate and place in the fridge. Strain the stock into an airtight container and let it chill in the fridge too.

5 Using a cleaver, chop the cold goose into 2 cm (¾ in) pieces, divide among plates and ladle over some masterstock. (If the masterstock has been used many times, it might become a little jelly-like when chilled because of the gelatine. Just warm it up a bit before serving.) Finish with a sprinkling of spring onion and coriander.

WE LOVE CHICKEN IN HONG KONG

Hong Kong people are fascinated with fresh poultry, and chicken remains an important part of traditional cooking in Hong Kong for special occasions or family celebrations like Chinese New Year.

As chicken is so revered in Hong Kong the cooking methods are taken very seriously and often require a lot of patience to get the desired result. Here are my tips for cooking chicken like a Hong Kong local.

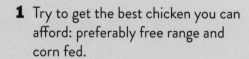

1 Try to get the best chicken you can afford: preferably free range and corn fed.

2 One simple way to get a nice savoury flavour into chicken, especially a whole chicken, is to brine it. Put the whole chicken (say, 1.2 kg/2 lb 10 oz) in 5 per cent brine (this means 50 g/1¾ oz salt for every litre/quart of water) for 3–4 hours. This works particularly well if you're using a dry cooking method like roasting, as the brining gives the meat extra moisture.

3 Another way is salt and time. Simply sprinkle a generous amount of salt all over the chicken and leave, uncovered, in the fridge overnight. Even if you can only salt it for a few hours, you'll be surprised how much flavour it adds.

WHITE CUT CHICKEN

This dish is an excellent example of 'less is more'. The chicken is simply poached in water until the meat is moist and tender and the skin is smooth and 'crisp'. Because it isn't poached in a stock, the chicken is simply presenting its own flavour so the better quality the chicken, the tastier it will be. This is why we call it 'white' chicken, as white here means pure. If you think about it, the concept of steeping the chicken in this way is not too far off from sous vide. These chefs from the old days had no idea they were cooking with 'science'!

Serves 4

100 g (3½ oz) fine sea salt

1.2 kg (2 lb 10 oz) whole chicken, well washed

4 litres (4 quarts) iced water

Spring onion and ginger sauce (page 171) or good-quality light soy sauce, to serve (optional)

1 Dissolve the salt in 2 litres (2 quarts) water. Add the chicken and leave to soak for an hour. Drain and pat the chicken dry with paper towel.

2 In a saucepan that can fit the chicken, bring 2 litres (2 quarts) of water to the boil. Prepare 2 litres (2 quarts) iced water in a similar-sized container.

3 Put the chicken in the boiling water for 1 minute, then put it straight into the iced water. This step will tighten the skin.

4 Pour 2 litres (2 quarts) water into another saucepan, preferably deeper with a smaller diameter than the first pan. Bring to the boil over high heat, then reduce the heat to low.

5 Holding the neck of the chicken, lower the body into the water until fully submerged. Lift the chicken out of the liquid, then lower it back in again. Repeat the process five times. The purpose of this is to raise the internal temperature of the chicken to a similar temperature to the poaching liquid.

6 Leave the chicken in the pan and bring the poaching liquid to a simmer (around 80–85°C/ 175–185°F), then turn the heat off. Let the chicken sit in the liquid for 20 minutes.

7 Take the chicken out. Bring the stock to a simmer again, then return the chicken to the pan and poach for another 20 minutes.

8 Prepare another 2 litres (2 quarts) iced water in a container. Add the chicken and let it cool in the iced water for about 10 minutes. The result is beautifully moist meat and smooth skin.

9 Cut up the chicken with a cleaver. First, cut off the wings, then the legs and breast. Cut each leg into five pieces and cut each breast into five to seven pieces.

10 Serve with spring onion and ginger sauce, or simply with a light soy sauce.

Note

If you have a bit of time, you could stir-fry some spring (green) onion, ginger and red shallot and scatter them over the chicken before serving. Season with light soy sauce, or even better the sauce from Soy sauce chicken (page 142).

BASIC SALTED CHICKEN

Again, less is more. Try to use the best and freshest chicken you can, then let time do the work. You might be surprised with the result.

Serves 4

2 tablespoons fine sea salt

½ teaspoon ground white pepper

1.2 kg (2 lb 10 oz) whole chicken, well washed

1 Rub the salt and pepper all over the outside and inside of the chicken. Cover and let it sit in the fridge for 3 days.

2 Take the chicken out of the fridge and wash it thoroughly, then pat dry with paper towel. Put the chicken on a steamer tray or heatproof plate.

3 Pour 2 litres (2 quarts) water into a large wok or saucepan and bring to the boil. Add the chicken on the tray or plate, cover with a lid and steam for 25–30 minutes. Remove the chicken and cool slightly, then transfer to the fridge to cool completely.

4 Cut up the chicken with a cleaver. First, cut off the wings, then the legs and breast. Cut each leg into five pieces and cut each breast into five to seven pieces.

5 Serve at room temperature with your choice of sauce.

Note
You can replace the whole chicken with chicken wings if you prefer. Reduce the steaming time to 15–20 minutes.

HONG KONG-STYLE POACHED CHICKEN WITH SAND GINGER

This is another simple and clean-tasting way to prepare chicken, this time poached in a fragrant stock flavoured with sand ginger.

Serves 4

100 g (3½ oz) fine sea salt

1.2 kg (2 lb 10 oz) whole chicken, well washed

2 litres (2 quarts) iced water

1 teaspoon sand ginger powder (see glossary)

Spring onion and ginger sauce (page 171), to serve

steamed rice, to serve (optional)

Sand ginger poaching stock

180 g (6½ oz) sand ginger powder (see glossary)

250 ml (8½ fl oz/1 cup) fish sauce

2 star anise

2 whole cloves

10 white peppercorns

2 dried bay leaves

4 cm (1½ in) piece ginger, sliced

2 garlic cloves, lightly crushed

1 teaspoon fine sea salt

1 spring (green) onion, roughly chopped (or use any trimmings you have)

1 Dissolve the salt in 2 litres (2 quarts) water. Add the chicken and leave to soak for 10 minutes.

2 In a saucepan large enough to fit the chicken, bring 2 litres (2 quarts) water to the boil. Prepare the iced water in a similar-sized container.

3 Put the chicken in the boiling water for 1 minute, then put it straight into the iced water. This step will tighten the skin.

4 To make the poaching stock, pour 2 litres (2 quarts) water into a saucepan that will fit the chicken. Bring to the boil over high heat. Blend the sand ginger powder and fish sauce to a paste and stir into the boiling water Add the remaining ingredients and return to the boil, then reduce the heat to low.

5 Holding the neck of the chicken, lower the body into the water until fully submerged. Lift the chicken out of the liquid, then lower it back in again. Repeat the process five times. The purpose of this is to raise the internal temperature of the chicken to a similar temperature to the poaching liquid.

6 Leave the chicken in the pan and bring the poaching liquid to a simmer (around 80–85°C/ 175–185°F), then turn the heat off. Let the chicken sit in the liquid for 20 minutes.

7 Take the chicken out. Bring the stock to a simmer again, then return the chicken to the pan and poach for another 20 minutes.

8 Take the chicken out of the poaching liquid, transfer to a plate and cool to room temperature in the fridge before chopping.

9 Meanwhile, stir the sand ginger powder through the spring onion and ginger sauce. Serve with the chopped chicken, and some steamed rice (if you like).

Note
Another way to serve this is to put the chopped chicken in a heatproof shallow bowl. Bring the poaching liquid back to the boil, ladle it over the chicken, then pour the liquid back into the pan. Repeat this about ten times to warm up the chicken. Serve warm with the dipping sauce.

SPICY MALA CHICKEN HOTPOT

In some restaurants, either during the meal or after finishing the chicken, the server will add some stock to the wok. Customers then continue to cook the hotpot ingredients using the mala chicken soup base. This is very popular as it transforms one dish into two dining experiences.

Serves 4

1.2 kg (2 lb 10 oz) whole chicken, well washed (or chicken wings)

2 tablespoons canola oil (or other cooking oil)

6 garlic cloves, halved lengthways

10 red shallots, halved lengthways

2 tablespoons thickly sliced spring (green) onion, white part only

4 cm (1½ in) piece ginger, thinly sliced

1 tablespoon Sichaun peppercorns

1 teaspoon fennel seeds

3 tablespoons shaoxing rice wine

80 ml (2½ fl oz/⅓ cup) mala sauce (see Note)

1 tablespoon oyster sauce

1 red onion, roughly chopped

1 bunch Chinese celery (see glossary), sliced into 4 cm (1½ in) batons

10 dried bird's eye chillies

2 bird's eye chillies (optional)

3 tablespoons chicken stock (optional)

To serve

1 bunch spring (green) onions, sliced into batons

1 bunch coriander (cilantro) leaves, roughly chopped

Marinade

1½ tablespoons light soy sauce

1 teaspoon dark soy sauce

1 teaspoon caster (superfine) sugar

¼ teaspoon ground white pepper

1 tablespoon shaoxing rice wine

½ teaspoon sesame oil

2 teaspoons cornflour (cornstarch)

Note

Mala sauce is available from Asian supermarkets. It's a fiery condiment usually made from Sichuan peppercorns, garlic, ginger, shallot, fermented chilli paste, chilli oil and spices. *Ma* refers to the numbing sensation from eating Sichuan peppercorns and *la* means 'spicy'. If you don't have mala sauce, you could use 2 tablespoons spicy bean paste, 1 tablespoon ground fermented bean paste, 1 teaspoon sugar and 2 teaspoons toasted Sichuan peppercorns instead.

1 To make the marinade, combine all the ingredients in a glass or ceramic dish. Chop the chicken into 7.5 cm (3 in) pieces, add to the marinade and turn to coat well. Cover and marinate in the fridge for at least 4 hours or up to 24 hours.

2 Heat the oil in a large wok or non-stick saucepan over medium heat, add the garlic, shallot, the spring onion and ginger and stir-fry for 2 minutes or until fragrant and slightly softened. Add the Sichaun peppercorns and fennel seeds and cook for another 30 seconds.

3 Increase the heat to high and add the chicken. Cook, untouched, until the chicken has browned nicely (about 1 minute), then turn the chicken over and give everything a good stir. Pour in the shaoxing wine, mala and oyster sauces and mix well.

4 Add the red onion, Chinese celery, dried chilli and fresh chilli (if using). Reduce the heat to low, cover with a lid and cook for 15–20 minutes or until the chicken and vegetables are cooked through. Check occasionally during this time and add the chicken stock if it starts to look a bit dry.

5 Taste and adjust the seasoning if necessary. To serve, scatter over the spring onion batons and coriander.

SALTED BAKED CHICKEN

In traditional recipes for this dish, the chicken is marinated, wrapped in paper, and then placed in a wok and covered with rock salt that has been stir-fried until very hot (which is the main heat source to cook it through). The result is very succulent meat with a wonderful fragrance when you unwrap the paper, but because this method takes up a lot of time and space (a whole wok for each bird), very few restaurants prepare the chicken in this way anymore. My method here is much simpler than the traditional one, but still very tasty.

Serves 4

100 g (3½ oz) fine sea salt

1.2 kg (2 lb 10 oz) whole chicken, well washed

4 cm (1½ in) piece ginger, sliced

1 bunch spring (green) onions, sliced into batons

1 teaspoon sesame oil

Spring onion and ginger sauce (page 171), to serve (optional)

steamed rice, to serve (optional)

Spiced salt mix

1 tablespoon sand ginger powder (see glossary)

1 teaspoon Chinese five-spice

1 tablespoon fine sea salt

1 teaspoon caster (superfine) sugar

1 Dissolve the salt in 2 litres (2 quarts) water. Add the chicken and leave to soak for 1 hour. Drain and pat the chicken dry with paper towel.

2 Meanwhile, to make the spiced salt mix, combine all the ingredients in a small bowl.

3 Rub the salt mix all over the outside and inside of the chicken. Cover and let it sit in the fridge for at least 12 hours or up to 24 hours.

4 Preheat the oven to 160°C (320°F) and place a rack inside a roasting tin.

5 Put the ginger and spring onion inside the chicken, then put the chicken on the rack. (If you don't have a rack, use a layer of spring onions instead.) Lightly brush the chicken skin with sesame oil and roast for 40 minutes. Turn the heat off and let the chicken sit in the oven for another 10 minutes.

6 Let the chicken cool before chopping. Serve at room temperature with spring onion and ginger sauce if you like, or simply with rice.

Note

If you don't have an oven, you can cook the chicken in a rice cooker. Cut the chicken in half (you'll be cooking half at a time). Arrange the ginger and spring onion on the bottom of the rice cooker, put half the chicken on top, then cover and press the cooking button. It should take about 40 minutes. Repeat with the other half.

SOY SAUCE CHICKEN

While the quality of the chicken is critical for white cut chicken and salted baked chicken (see pages 134 and 141), for this dish, it's the soy sauce that's key.

Tau chau is a first-press soy sauce you can get in Hong Kong. Similar to extra-virgin olive oil, tau chau is the very first extract of soy sauce from the first round of fermentation. Each tank of fermented beans only has one round of production, so this soy sauce is rare and expensive. Here, I use a mixture of light and dark soy sauce, but feel free to use tau chau if you can get your hands on some.

Serves 4

100 g (3½ oz) fine sea salt

1.2 kg (2 lb 10 oz) chicken wings, well washed

2 litres (2 quarts) iced water

20 g (¾ oz) yellow rock sugar

1 tablespoon rose wine

shredded spring onion greens, to serve

Soy sauce stock

750 ml (25½ fl oz/3 cups) light soy sauce

3 tablespoons dark soy sauce

150 g (5½ oz) yellow rock sugar

125 ml (4 fl oz/½ cup) rosé wine

10 red shallots, peeled

10 slices ginger

5 spring (green) onions, sliced into batons

1 Dissolve the salt in 2 litres (2 quarts) water. Add the chicken wings and leave to soak for 1 hour. Drain and pat the wings dry with paper towel.

2 In a medium saucepan, bring 2 litres (2 quarts) water to the boil. Prepare the iced water in a similar-sized container.

3 Put the wings in the boiling water for 1 minute, then put them straight into the iced water for 5 minutes before draining. This step will tighten the skin.

4 Combine all the ingredients for the soy sauce stock with 750 ml (25½ fl oz/3 cups) water in a medium wok or saucepan and bring to the boil, stirring occasionally until the rock sugar has dissolved. Reduce the heat to low and simmer for 5 minutes.

5 Turn the heat to high then add the wings. Bring to the boil, then turn off the heat and let the wings sit in the stock for 10 minutes.

6 Turn the heat back to medium for 1–2 minutes, until the stock is steaming again, then turn off the heat and let the wings sit in the stock for another 10 minutes.

7 Drain the wings, reserving the stock liquid and aromatics. Transfer the wings to a tray and place in the fridge to cool to room temperature.

8 Meanwhile, pour 250 ml (8½ fl oz/1 cup) of the reserved stock into a small saucepan along with the reserved shallot, ginger and spring onion. Bring the liquid to simmer. Add the rock sugar and stir until dissolved, then pour in the wine and turn the heat off.

9 Serve the chicken wings topped with the hot soy stock and spring onion greens.

LEMON CHICKEN

Sweet and sour pork is a well-known crowd pleaser around the world, but this dish is up there in popularity, too. The sauce is made with lots of lemon juice, and is not thickened with cornflour, making it lighter and fresher – the perfect foil for the oiliness of the fried chicken. I hope you like it.

Serves 4

4 boneless chicken thighs

2 tablespoons white sesame seeds

150 g (5½ oz) fry powder (see Note), plus extra for dusting

2 litres (2 quarts) canola oil (or other cooking oil)

lemon slices, to serve

Brine

140 g (5 oz) fine sea salt

2 tablespoons caster (superfine) sugar

1 whole clove

1 teaspoon black peppercorns

zest of 1 lemon

Lemon sauce

3 tablespoons liquid glucose

3 tablespoons light soy sauce

80 g (2¾ oz) yellow rock sugar

zest of 1 lemon

1 slice ginger

1 small piece kombu seaweed

125 ml (4 fl oz/½ cup) lemon juice

1 To make the brine, combine all the ingredients and 1 litre (1 quart/4 cups) water in a medium saucepan and bring to a simmer. Remove and let it cool in the fridge.

2 Add the chicken thighs to the brine, making sure they are fully submerged, then set aside in the fridge for 2 hours. Remove the thighs and pat dry with paper towel, then cut each one into five even pieces.

3 Preheat the oven to 160°C (320°F) and line a baking tray with baking paper.

4 Spread the sesame seeds over the prepared tray in an even layer and bake for 15 minutes or until golden brown. Remove and set aside.

5 To make the lemon sauce, combine the glucose, soy sauce, sugar, lemon zest, ginger and 3 tablespoons water in a saucepan over medium heat. Bring to a simmer and cook for about 20 minutes or until reduced by one-third. Remove from the heat and stir in the kombu and lemon juice. Set aside to cool to room temperature.

6 Whisk the fry powder and 250 ml (8½ fl oz/1 cup) water in a bowl to form a smooth batter. Place in the fridge until you are ready to use it.

7 Pour the oil into a large saucepan and heat over high heat to 180°C (350°F) or until a cube of bread dropped in the oil browns in 15 seconds.

8 Dust the chicken pieces in the extra fry powder, shaking off the excess, then place in the batter, allowing the excess to drip off. Add half the chicken to the oil and fry for 5 minutes or until cooked and golden. Remove with a slotted spoon and place in a mixing bowl. Repeat with the remaining chicken.

9 Add the lemon sauce and half the toasted sesame seeds to the chicken and mix together. You want every piece to be evenly coated in the sauce and seeds. Transfer to a serving dish with some lemon slices and sprinkle over the remaining sesame seeds.

Note

Fry powder is similar to tempura flour and can be purchased at Asian grocery stores. If you can't find it use a home-made mix of 75 g (2¾ oz/½ cup) plain (all-purpose) flour, 60 g (2 oz/½ cup) cornflour (cornstarch) and 1 teaspoon baking powder.

KUNG PO CHICKEN

Along with sweet and sour pork and lemon chicken, kung po chicken is probably one of the most popular Chinese dishes, not only in Hong Kong, or in Sichuan (its place of origin), but also in many Western countries. Compared with the Sichuan style of cooking, kung po chicken in Hong Kong is more Westernised, modified to be less mouth-numbingly spicy to suit the local palate.

Serves 4

2 tablespoons light soy sauce

2 tablespoons shaoxing rice wine

½ teaspoon ground white pepper

1 tablespoon cornflour (cornstarch)

600 g (1 lb 5 oz) boneless chicken thighs, cut into 2.5 cm (1 in) cubes

165 ml (5½ fl oz) canola oil (or other cooking oil)

5 spring (green) onions, white part only, cut into bite-sized pieces

2 long red chillies, roughly chopped

4 dried long red chillies, roughly chopped

2 celery stalks (use the tender inner stalks), cut into bite-sized pieces (reserve any leaves for garnish)

1 yellow bell pepper (capsicum), cut into bite-sized pieces

1 red bell pepper (capsicum), cut into bite-sized pieces

1–2 bird's eye chillies, chopped (optional, if you like it spicier)

50 g (1¾ oz/1/3 cup) toasted peanuts

Kung po sauce

1 tablespoon Sichuan chilli bean paste

2 tablespoons ketchup

1 tablespoon Chinkiang black vinegar

100 ml (3½ fl oz) light soy sauce

2 tablespoons caster (superfine) sugar

½ teaspoon Sichuan peppercorns, toasted and ground

1 teaspoon grated ginger

1 Combine the soy sauce, shaoxing wine and white pepper in a glass or ceramic dish. Add the chicken and turn to coat, then cover and marinate in the fridge for at least 3 hours, preferably overnight. Just before cooking, toss the chicken in the cornflour, shaking off the excess.

2 To make the sauce, combine all the ingredients and 125 ml (4 fl oz/½ cup) water in a small bowl or jug. It should taste salty, sweet and a little bit spicy.

3 Heat 125 ml (4 fl oz/½ cup) of the oil in a large wok over high heat, add the chicken and leave untouched for 30 seconds so it has time to brown. Turn the pieces over and cook for another 30 seconds. Stir and break the chicken pieces up a little bit, then cook for another 2 minutes or until they are nearly cooked through. Remove with a slotted spoon and drain on paper towel.

4 Pour the used oil out of the wok (you can strain and reuse it if you like). Wipe out the wok, then pour in the remaining 2 tablespoons oil and heat over high heat. Add the spring onion and fresh and dried red chilli and toss for 10 seconds. Add the celery and bell pepper and quickly stir-fry just until the vegetables have a nice char. Return the chicken to the wok and toss for another 30 seconds.

5 Add 250 ml (8½ fl oz/1 cup) of the sauce and cook for 1 minute or until it is glossy and slightly thickened without reducing too much. If you feel it has reduced too much or tastes too strong add a splash of water; if it tastes good but isn't saucy enough add a little more sauce. For those who like it spicy, now is the time to add the bird's eye chilli.

6 Throw in the toasted peanuts, give everything a quick toss and serve immediately garnished with celery leaves, if you have some.

TOMATO AND EGG STIR-FRY

I know tomato and egg might seem like an odd combination, but they go together so well in a stir-fry. Cheap, simple and full of nostalgia, this is a childhood dish that most Hong Kong mums cook at home. It can be tricky to achieve a good tomato flavour – you're after a well-balanced sweet, savoury and tangy sauce to coat the fluffy eggs. When it is done well, it tastes great on a bed of steaming hot rice!

Serves 2

2 vine-ripened tomatoes

3 eggs

¼ teaspoon fine sea salt

2 tablespoons canola oil (or other cooking oil)

½ onion, sliced

2 slices ginger

2 red shallots, roughly chopped

1 garlic clove, roughly chopped

25 g (1 oz) Chinese brown sugar (or soft brown sugar)

3 tablespoons ketchup

1 teaspoon light soy sauce

1 teaspoon Worcestershire sauce

¼ teaspoon dark soy sauce

1 tablespoon chopped spring (green) onion

1 tablespoon chopped coriander (cilantro) leaves

1 Cut each tomato in half lengthways, then cut each half into three slices.

2 Whisk together the eggs and salt in a bowl.

3 Heat a medium wok or non-stick frying pan over high heat until hot. Add 1 tablespoon of oil, then reduce the heat to low and pour in the egg mixture. Cook, stirring, until the egg is nearly cooked. Transfer the scrambled egg to a bowl.

4 Wipe out the pan and return it to low heat. Add the remaining oil, then the onion and ginger and stir-fry for 30 seconds. Add the shallot and garlic and stir-fry for another 30 seconds. Toss in the tomato and stir-fry for another 2 minutes, then stir through the brown sugar. Add 125 ml (4 fl oz/½ cup) of water and simmer for 3 minutes.

5 Pour in the ketchup and light soy sauce and cook for another 5 minutes. The tomato will start to release its juices, helping the mixture to form a sauce. Add the Worcestershire sauce and dark soy sauce, then the scrambled egg and stir for another 30 seconds. During this time the egg will finish cooking and thicken the sauce.

6 Remove from the heat, sprinkle with the spring onion and coriander and serve immediately.

GU LO YUK

Sweet and sour pork

From all-you-can eat food courts to full-service restaurants, sweet and sour pork is a popular choice. The key to this dish is, unsurprisingly, the perfect balance of sweetness and sourness, and the sauce should be just thick enough to coat all the ingredients, leaving the pork crispy on the outside and juicy on the inside.

Serves 4

1 kg (2 lb 3 oz) pork ribs, cut into 4 cm (1½ in) cubes

2 litres (2 quarts) canola oil (or other cooking oil)

cornflour (cornstarch), for coating

½ onion, diced

½ red bell pepper (capsicum), diced

½ green bell pepper (capsicum), diced

½ yellow bell pepper (capsicum), diced

2 garlic cloves, sliced

3 tablespoons shaoxing rice wine

375 ml (2½ fl oz/1½ cups) Sweet and sour sauce (page 173)

12–16 pieces diced tinned pineapple

steamed rice, to serve

Marinade

1 small egg

1 teaspoon fine sea salt

1 teaspoon caster (superfine) sugar

¼ teaspoon ground white pepper

1 tablespoon light soy sauce

1 tablespoon shaoxing rice wine

1 tablespoon cornflour (cornstarch)

1 tablespoon plain (all-purpose) flour

2 teaspoons vegetable oil

1 Rinse the pork and pat dry. This is important – if you don't dry the pork thoroughly, it will affect the crispness later on when you fry it.

2 To make the marinade, combine all the ingredients, except the oil, in a large glass or ceramic dish. Add the pork and turn to coat in the marinade. Leave it for 1–2 minutes, then add the oil and mix well.

3 Pour the cooking oil into a large wok or heavy-based saucepan over medium heat and bring it up to about 160°C (320°F) or until a cube of bread dropped in the oil browns in 30–35 seconds.

4 Meanwhile, lightly coat the pork pieces with cornflour, shaking off the excess.

5 Carefully lower the pork into the oil and fry, untouched, for 1 minute. You don't want to move it around otherwise the flour coating might drop off. After a minute, gently stir the oil so the pieces loosen up naturally, then continue to fry for another 3 minutes. Remove the pork with a slotted spoon.

6 Increase the heat to high and bring the oil temperature up to 190°C (375°F) or until a cube of bread dropped in the oil browns in 10 seconds. Return the pork to the oil and fry for another 30–60 seconds until golden brown and very crispy. Remove the pork and pour off all but 1 tablespoon of the oil.

7 Reheat the oil over medium heat, add the onion and saute for 30 seconds, then add the bell pepper and cook for another 30 seconds. Add the garlic and stir-fry for another 30 seconds. Pour in the shaoxing wine and the sweet and sour sauce and bring to the boil. Add the pineapple and simmer for 10 seconds.

8 Add the fried pork to the sauce, then immediately remove from the heat and keep stirring. There should be just enough sauce to coat all the ingredients. Serve immediately. With rice of course!

STEAMED MINCED PORK WITH SHIITAKE

Growing up in Hong Kong, I remember eating this dish quite a lot at home and in restaurants. Steamed minced (ground) pork is not commonly found in other Asian cuisines; rather it is a very comforting 'home' food among Hong Kong families. In this basic but versatile dish, minced pork can be used alone or mixed with other ingredients such as dried squid, preserved cabbage, salted fish or salted eggs.

Instead of buying minced pork, in which the structure of the meat has already been broken down too much, it is far better to buy pork meat and chop it by hand. It will make a huge difference to the texture and flavour.

Serves 2–3

5 dried shiitake mushrooms

1 tablespoon light soy sauce

500 g (1 lb 2 oz) pork collar butt (or pork shoulder butt), skin off

steamed rice, to serve

Seasoning

1 teaspoon finely chopped garlic

1 teaspoon finely chopped ginger

1 tablespoon shaoxing rice wine

1 tablespoon cornflour (cornstarch)

1 tablespoon light soy sauce

1 tablespoon oyster sauce

¼ teaspoon fine sea salt

¼ teaspoon caster (superfine) sugar

⅛ teaspoon ground white pepper

1 Soak the dried shiitake in 500 ml (17 fl oz/2 cups) tepid water for 6 hours or overnight. Remove the mushrooms and reserve the soaking water. Strain it through a fine sieve to remove any dirt or sand.

2 Combine the rehydrated shiitake, soaking liquid and light soy sauce in a medium saucepan. Bring to the boil, then reduce the heat and simmer for 30 minutes. Take out the mushrooms and finely dice them. Reserve the cooking liquid.

3 Soak the pork collar in water for 15 minutes to release any excess blood. Drain and rinse well, then pat dry. Separate the pork fat from the lean meat, then finely dice them separately.

4 Put the lean meat on a chopping board. Using a cleaver, finely chop the pork in one direction for about 1 minute, then turn the board 90 degrees and chop for another minute. Put the pork fat in the middle and repeat the chopping action to mince the fat. The result will be finely minced meat and fat that still retains some texture (unlike machine-minced pork).

5 Combine all the seasoning ingredients and 80 ml (2½ fl oz/⅓ cup) of the reserved shiitake cooking liquid in a bowl.

6 Place the minced pork in a medium bowl and add half the seasoning liquid. Mix with a clean hand for 1 minute or until the seasoning liquid is fully absorbed. Add the rest of the seasoning and mix for another minute. By now the seasoning should be fully absorbed and the meat should feel sticky. Using your hand, lightly smash the mixture into the bowl a few times (this will create a more 'bouncy' texture when the meat is cooked). Mix in the diced shiitake.

7 Put the mixture in the fridge for 30 minutes.

8 Pour water into a large saucepan to a depth of about 3 cm (1¼ in) and bring to the boil. Spread out the pork mixture on a heatproof plate and make a small hole in the middle of the meat. Cover and steam for 8–10 minutes or until the juices in the hole run clear.

9 Serve immediately with freshly cooked rice.

MORNING GLORY WITH FERMENTED BEANCURD AND CHILLI

If you're feeling adventurous, fermented beancurd is a great authentic local condiment to try. It's somewhat similar to cheese, with a strong flavour due to the fermentation. In less affluent times in Hong Kong, people would often have a simple meal of plain congee with a cube of fermented beancurd. Like Vegemite in Australia, it can also be spread on a piece of hot bread!

If you can't find morning glory (also known as water spinach or kangkong) at your local markets, fermented beancurd also goes well with lettuce. And if you like it spicy feel free to add some bird's eye chilli.

Serves 4

1 bunch (about 500 g/1 lb 2 oz) morning glory (water spinach)

3 tablespoons canola oil (or other cooking oil)

2 tablespoons roughly chopped garlic

1 long red chilli, deseeded and thinly sliced

80 g (2¾ oz) fermented beancurd

½ teaspoon caster (superfine) sugar

½ teaspoon fish sauce

1 Cut the morning glory into 8–10 cm (3–4 in) lengths, then wash well and trim off any dry stems or wilted leaves. Drain off the excess water.

2 Heat the oil in a large frying pan over high heat, add the garlic and saute for 10 seconds or until it starts to turn lightly golden, then add the chilli and saute for 30 seconds.

3 Add the fermented beancurd and give it a good stir. Add the morning glory, then the sugar and fish sauce and cook for 3–5 minutes until the stems are just tender. Transfer to a plate and serve.

STAR FERRY

STIR-FRY KING

Invented by a very popular store in Sham Shui Po, this dish uses quality ingredients like sun-dried prawns (shrimp), fresh prawns and flowering garlic chives. The power of the wok and high heat help to bring out the flavour of these premium ingredients during the stir-frying process. Great with rice and a glass of chilled beer.

Serves 2

100 g (3½ oz) large dried prawns (shrimp) (see Note)

1 bunch (300 g/10½ oz) flowering garlic chives

1 tablespoon canola oil (or other cooking oil)

100 g (3½ oz) fresh prawns (shrimp), peeled and deveined

4 red shallots, thinly sliced

2 garlic cloves, finely chopped

pinch of fine sea salt

1 tablespoon shaoxing rice wine

50 g (1¾ oz/⅓ cup) cashews, toasted

Finishing sauce

1 tablespoon oyster sauce

2 teaspoons light soy sauce

1 teaspoon cornflour (cornstarch)

¼ teaspoon ground white pepper

1 Soak the dried prawns in water for 30 minutes or until rehydrated, then drain.

2 To make the finishing sauce, combine all the ingredients and 80 ml (2½ fl oz/⅓ cup) water in a small bowl or jug.

3 Trim about 4 cm (1½ in) off the base of the chives as this part is generally too woody. Wash thoroughly, then cut into 5 cm (2 in) lengths.

4 Heat a large wok over heat, add the dried prawns and pan-fry for 1 minute. Add the oil, then turn the prawns over and cook for another minute. Remove and set aside.

5 Add the fresh prawns and cook on one side for 30 seconds to give them a nice colour, then turn them over and fry for another 30 seconds until cooked through. Remove and set aside.

6 Add the shallot and garlic and stir-fry for 20 seconds. Toss in the garlic chives and stir-fry for about 1 minute to achieve a nice char. Season with the salt. Return the dried and fresh prawns to the wok and stir-fry for 30 seconds, then stir in the shaoxing wine.

7 Give the finishing sauce a stir, then slowly pour it into the wok, stir-frying all the while until the flavours of the prawns and garlic chives marry together and the sauce thickens slightly. Add the cashews and toss for 10 seconds, then serve immediately.

Note

Large dried prawns (shrimp) are a higher-quality ingredient than the more common small dried shrimp you find in big bags in Asian supermarkets. The top-quality dried prawns are carefully semi sun-dried by hand and the higher the grade, the larger they are. Ask your Asian grocer – if unavailable, substitute with the smaller variety, but get the best quality you can.

SHA LA GWAT

'Salad' ribs

Sha la gwat literally means 'salad' ribs, or fried pork ribs with salad sauce, in English. Created by a Hong Kong chef in the 1970s, the secret of this dish is to mix mayonnaise with condensed milk, giving the ribs a touch of sweetness as well as a sour–savoury flavour. Sounds strange, but it really is delicious.

Serves 2

500 g (1 lb 2 oz) pork ribs, cut into individual ribs

cornflour (cornstarch), for coating

250 ml (8½ fl oz/1 cup) canola oil (or other cooking oil)

3 tablespoons mayonnaise

2 teaspoons sweetened condensed milk

sliced red chilli, to garnish

Marinade

1 teaspoon light soy sauce

½ teaspoon fine sea salt

1 teaspoon caster (superfine) sugar

1 teaspoon shaoxing rice wine

½ teaspoon ground white pepper

1 teaspoon cornflour (cornstarch)

1 teaspoon vegetable oil

1 tablespoon curry powder

1 Soak the pork ribs in lightly salted water for 15 minutes.

2 Meanwhile, to make the marinade, mix together all the ingredients in a large glass or ceramic dish.

3 Drain the ribs and rinse well, then pat dry with paper towel. Add to the marinade and turn to coat well, then cover and marinate in the fridge for at least 4 hours or overnight. Take them out of the fridge 1 hour before cooking to bring to room temperature. Coat the ribs in cornflour, dusting off the excess.

4 Pour the oil into a large deep frying pan and heat over high heat to 160°C (320°F) or until a cube of bread dropped in the oil browns in 30–35 seconds. Reduce the heat to medium, add the ribs one by one and cook for 2 minutes each side. Depending on the size of the ribs, the total cooking time could range from 15–20 minutes. The best way to check is to cut into the meat of the largest rib.

5 When the ribs are cooked through, increase the heat to high to give them a nice colour. Remove and drain on paper towel.

6 Mix together the mayonnaise and condensed milk.

7 Transfer the hot ribs to a large bowl, add the mayonnaise mixture and toss to coat evenly. Serve immediately, garnished with sliced chilli.

SWEET TARO BALLS

Texture, texture, and texture! One of the key features of Cantonese cuisine is having a range of textures in a dish or a meal. Different from the Cantonese glutinous rice balls (*tong yuen*), chewy, springy *wu yuen* are made without a filling and are tinted by the natural colouring of the ingredients (here we use taro for a purplish colour, but orange sweet potato gives a vivid yellow colour).

These are delicious served in a sweet soup of coconut syrup.

Make 20–30 small balls

80 g (3 oz) purple taro or sweet potato, peeled and thinly sliced

45 g (1½ oz) tapioca flour, plus 200 g (7 oz) extra, for coating

30 ml (1 fl oz) boiling water

iced water, to refresh

2 teaspoons caster (superfine) sugar

Coconut syrup (see page 101), optional

1 Pour water into a medium saucepan to a depth of about 3 cm (1¼ in) and bring to the boil. Arrange the sweet potato slices on a steamer tray or plate (without overlapping), then cover and steam for 20–30 minutes or until completely soft.

2 Mash the sweet potato with a potato masher or fork until there are no big lumps – you won't get it completely smooth. Add the tapioca flour and mix well. Pour in the boiling water and let it sit for 30 seconds. Stir with a fork until the mixture starts to come together, then knead in the bowl to form a dough.

3 Transfer the dough to a clean bench (no need to add any flour) and knead for about 3 minutes until nice and smooth. Roll the dough into a 1 cm (½ in) thick cylinder and cut into 2 cm (¾ in) pieces.

4 Tip the extra tapioca flour into a medium bowl, add the dough and shake the bowl so each piece is coated.

5 Bring about 2 litres (2 quarts) water to the boil in a medium saucepan and prepare a bowl of iced water.

6 Drop the dough balls into the boiling water and cook for about 1 minute or until they float to the surface. Drain and refresh in the iced water.

7 Drain into a bowl and toss through the sugar to prevent sticking. If you like, serve the balls into dessert bowls topped with coconut syrup.

TONG YUEN

Glutinous rice balls with black sesame

As I have mentioned before, Hong Kong people like to have dishes that represent good fortune. Glutinous rice balls (or sweet dumplings) are known as *tong yuen* in Cantonese, which means 'gather together'. These chewy delights are often made and served during Chinese New Year, at weddings or other family celebrations. I use a black sesame filling here but they are also delicious filled with with red bean or peanuts.

Makes 12

40 g (1½ oz) Chinese brown sugar or soft brown sugar

2 slices ginger (optional)

Filling

100 g (3½ oz/⅔ cup) black sesame seeds

60 g (2 oz) caster (superfine) sugar

65 g (2¼ oz) butter, softened

Dough

150 g (5½ oz) glutinous rice flour

35 ml (1¼ fl oz) boiling water

1 To make the filling, heat a medium frying pan over medium heat for 1 minute, then reduce the heat to low. Add the sesame seeds and toast, shaking the pan and stirring constantly, for 5–10 minutes or until fragrant. (It can be hard to tell if the seeds are ready because of the colour, but if you have toasted white sesame seeds, take note of the timing and apply it to the black seeds. Essentially you want them to smell nice and toasty, but not burnt.

2 Tip the warm seeds into a blender or small food processor and blend to a fine paste. Allow to cool slightly, then add the sugar, then the butter and mix until well combined. Place in the fridge for at least 30 minutes to firm up.

3 Portion the dough into 12 even balls. You could use a melon baller to do this, otherwise put some food-handling gloves on and roll them by hand.

4 To make the dough, put the glutinous rice flour in a bowl, add the boiling water and mix with a fork. Pour in 80 ml (2½ fl oz/⅓ cup) tepid water and mix with a spoon until the dough starts to come together, then knead in the bowl to form a dough. Cover tightly with plastic wrap and leave to rest for 5 minutes.

5 Transfer the dough to a clean bench (no need to add any flour) and roll it into a 1 cm (½ in) thick cylinder. Cut into 12 even pieces and roll each piece into a ball. The balls dry very quickly when exposed to air, so as you finish each ball, place it on a tray and cover the tray with plastic wrap or a damp tea towel before continuing with the next.

6 Press each rice ball into a flat round, then pick it up and form it into a bowl shape, making the edges a bit thinner as they will be pressed together to enclose the filling. Remember to work with one at a time and return them to the covered tray as you go.

7 Put a ball of sesame filling into each 'bowl', then gently fold the dough over to enclose the filling. Make sure there aren't any holes or that the dough hasn't been stretched too thinly, otherwise the filling might come out when the rice balls are boiled. If the dough seems a bit dry, dip your finger into some water and gently moisten it.

8 Dissolve the brown sugar into 250 ml (8½ fl oz/1 cup) water and add the ginger slices, if using.

9 Pour about 2 litres (2 quarts) water into a medium saucepan and bring to the boil over high heat. Add the rice balls one by one, trying not to let them stick to the bottom of the pan, and boil for 3–4 minutes or until they float to the surface. Scoop them out with a slotted spoon and divide among bowls (or combine in one serving bowl), then ladle over the brown sugar soup. Serve hot.

Note

You can make the glutinous rice balls ahead of time and store them, uncooked, in the freezer. Cook from frozen.

BAS

ICS

XO SAUCE

Named after a popular alcohol (extra old cognac), XO means deluxe. The sauce was created in Hong Kong in the 1980s, using luxury ingredients like dried scallop and Jinhua ham. This sauce is expensive not only because of the ingredients used, but also the time and attention required to make it. As is often the case, when you put a lot of effort into something you are rewarded with a great result. XO sauce is no exception.

Makes 1.5 litres (1½ quarts)

50 g (1¾ oz) dried shrimp

200 g (7 oz) dried scallop

20 g (¾ oz) salted fish

600 ml (20½ fl oz) vegetable oil

250 g (9 oz) red shallots, thinly sliced

250 g (9 oz) garlic cloves, thinly sliced

30 g (1 oz) dried red chillies

100 g (3½ oz) Jinhua ham
(see glossary), diced

50 g (1¾ oz) long red chillies

2 spring (green) onions, white part only, sliced

30 g (1 oz) sweet bean paste

30 g (1 oz) caster (superfine) sugar

fine sea salt

Notes
The oil needs to be hot when you start adding the shallot and garlic. All the ingredients need to be fried, not confit.

It's important to add the ingredients in the order stated in the method and cook for the specified time, especially at the end. You don't want the sauce to be under or overcooked.

Keep stirring otherwise the ingredients will catch on the bottom of the wok and burn.

1 Preheat the oven to 170°C (340°F).

2 Soak the dried shrimp in 200 ml (7 fl oz) water for 30 minutes. Drain the shrimp and transfer to a baking tray. Place in the oven for 10–15 minutes to dry out. Set aside.

3 Soak the dried scallop in 400 ml (13½ fl oz) water for 30 minutes. Remove the scallop and reserve the soaking water. Break the scallop into threads. Pour the soaking water into a small saucepan and bring to a gentle simmer.

4 Soak the salted fish in 100 ml (3½ fl oz) water for 30 minutes. Drain, then finely dice.

5 Heat the oil in a large wok over high heat to 180°C (350°F) or until a cube of bread dropped in the oil browns in 15 seconds. Add the scallop (be careful as the oil will bubble up) and fry for about 5 minutes or until crisp. Strain, then return the oil to the wok and heat to 200°C (400°F) or until a cube of bread browns in 5 seconds.

6 Add the shallot, closely followed by the garlic and fry just until lightly golden. Add the dried chilli and cook, stirring, for 2 minutes.

7 Add the shrimp and ham and fry for about 5 minutes, then add the fresh chilli and salted fish and fry for another 5 minutes, stirring regularly.

8 Add spring onion, sweet bean paste, sugar, fried scallops and hot reserved scallop water, and a pinch of salt and cook, stirring occasionally, for 5 minutes or until fragrant, the water has evaporated and the ingredients are a deep red colour (almost like char siu). Remove from the heat and set aside to cool slightly

9 You can leave it chunky or blend it to a smoother consistency – it's entirely up to you. Store in an airtight container in the fridge for up to 1 month.

MASTERSTOCK

This staple stock is usually made with soy sauce, rock sugar and shaoxing rice wine flavoured with spices and aromatics such as ginger and spring (green) onions. It is designed to be used repeatedly to poach or braise meat, the flavour improving with every use.

Makes 4 litres (4 quarts)

60 g (2 oz) ginger, lightly smashed with a cleaver

125 ml (4 fl oz/½ cup) canola or other cooking oil

1.5 litres (1½ quarts) light soy sauce

190 ml (6½ fl oz) dark soy sauce

600 g (1 lb 5 oz) yellow rock sugar

20 g (¾ oz) fine sea salt

160 ml (5½ fl oz) shaoxing rice wine

200 g (7 oz) red rice (optional)

35 g (1¼ oz) star anise

35 g (1¼ oz) cassia bark

35 g (1¼ oz) dried liquorice root (see glossary)

10 g (¼ oz) black cardamom pods

10 g (¼ oz) Sichuan peppercorns

10 g (¼ oz) cloves

10 g (¼ oz) sand ginger powder (see glossary)

1 piece dried mandarin peel

1 Lightly fry the ginger in the oil for 1 minute. Remove with a slotted spoon. Reserve the flavoured oil for another use.

2 Place the ginger in a large saucepan or stockpot, add the remaining ingredients and 3 litres (3 quarts) water and bring to the boil over high heat. Reduce the heat and simmer for 1 hour. Remove and set aside to cool completely.

3 Strain and pour into an airtight container, then closely cover the top with plastic wrap to prevent water condensation and mould forming. Store in the fridge. Stored properly like this, it will keep indefinitely and the flavour will get better and better.

4 When you are ready to cook with it, bring it to the boil and top up the spices every time you use it.

SPRING ONION AND GINGER SAUCE

This is the best thing to serve with chicken, especially white cut chicken. It's funny, if you've grown up with this sauce (as I have) it feels like you're eating chicken even if the sauce is being served with other meat! Or is that just me?

Makes 125 ml (4 fl oz/½ cup)

60 g (2 oz/⅓ cup) grated ginger

½ bunch spring (green) onion, white parts finely chopped, green parts thinly sliced

2 teaspoons fine sea salt

80 ml (2½ fl oz/⅓ cup) vegetable oil

1 Mix together the ginger, spring onion whites and salt in a small heatproof bowl.

2 Heat the oil in a small saucepan until smoking hot, then pour over the ginger mixture and stir to combine. Mix in the spring onion greens and serve.

3 This sauce will keep in an airtight container in the fridge for up to 1 week.

SWEET AND SOUR SAUCE

Makes 1 litre (1 quart/4 cups)

100 g (3½ oz) yellow rock sugar

200 g (7 oz) Chinese brown sugar or soft brown sugar

1 lemon, halved

500 ml (17 fl oz/2 cups) rice wine vinegar

1 tablespoon fine sea salt

200 g (7 oz) ketchup

80 ml (2½ fl oz/⅓ cup) Worcestershire sauce

1 teaspoon dark soy sauce

1 Dissolve the rock sugar and brown sugar in 250 ml (8½ fl oz/1 cup) water in a small bowl. Squeeze the lemon juice into the mixture and stir.

2 Pour the rice wine vinegar into a medium glass or enamelled cast-iron saucepan (the sauce is too acidic for a metal pan). Bring the vinegar to the boil, add the salt and mix until it has dissolved. Strain in the sugar and lemon water (if some of the sugar still hasn't dissolved, return it to the heat until it has). Stir in the sauces. Bring the mixture to the boil, then reduce the heat and simmer for 5 minutes. Remove the pan from the heat and taste the sauce. It should be sweet and sour with a background savoury note. Adjust the flavour with sugar, vinegar and salt if needed.

3 Let the sauce cool, then store in an airtight container in the fridge for up to 2 weeks. Just make sure you use a clean, dry spoon or ladle to take the sauce out.

CHILLI OIL

**Makes about 500 ml
(17 fl oz/2 cups)**

600 ml (20½ fl oz) canola oil
(or other cooking oil)

10 garlic cloves, lightly smashed

100 g (3½ oz) ginger, sliced

10 red shallots, sliced

3 spring (green) onions, sliced

5 tablespoons chilli flakes

3 dried bird's eye chillies

1 tablespoon Sichuan peppercorns

1 Pour 200 ml (7 fl oz) of the oil into a medium saucepan and heat over high heat until really hot. Reduce the heat to medium, add the garlic, ginger, shallot and spring onion and cook for 5 minutes or until fragrant and slightly coloured.

2 Add the chilli flakes, dried chillies and peppercorns, reduce the heat to low and cook for another 2 minutes or until fragrant and the bright red colour of the chilli becomes a deep red (indicating it is well roasted). Add another 200 ml (7 fl oz) of the oil to bring the heat down slightly, then continue to cook until the vegetables are lightly golden, about 5 minutes. Pour in the remaining oil, increase the heat to high and cook until golden brown.

3 Remove from the heat and leave to cool completely. Strain the chilli oil into a clean jar, discarding the solids. Store in the fridge for up to 4 weeks.

DUMPLING DIPPING SAUCE

**Makes about 250 ml
(8½ fl oz/1 cup)**

3 tablespoons Chinkiang black vinegar

70 ml (2¼ fl oz) light soy sauce

1 tablespoon caster (superfine) sugar

1 Place all the ingredients and 100 ml (3½ fl oz) water in a small bowl and mix until the sugar has dissolved. Pour into a clean jar and store in the fridge for up to 2 weeks.

Note

For extra flavour, toast spices such as star anise, clove or fennel seeds and infuse in the water for 30 minutes. Strain and add to the sauce.

You can also add fresh ingredients just before serving. Try some sliced fresh chilli or chilli oil, chopped garlic, ginger, spring (green) onion or coriander (cilantro) leaves.

SUPREME BROTH

Usually made with chicken, lean pork meat and/or Jinhau ham, this flavourful stock will enhance any dish you use it in. Serve it as a soup or as a base stock to replace water for extra depth of flavour.

Makes about 1.5 litres (1½ quarts)

5 dried shiitake mushrooms

1 litre (1 quart/4 cups) chicken stock

200 g (7 oz) chicken wings

100 g (3½ oz) Jinhua ham (see glossary)

20 g dried scallop

5 dried red dates (see glossary)

2 slices ginger

light soy sauce, for seasoning

1 Soak the dried shiitake in 500 ml (17 fl oz/2 cups) tepid water for 6 hours or overnight. Remove the shiitake and reserve the soaking water. Strain through a fine sieve to remove any dirt or sand.

2 Pour the soaking liquid into a clean pan, add all the remaining ingredients (except the soy sauce) and bring to simmer over medium heat, skimming off any impurities on the surface. Simmer for 1 hour, then remove from the heat, cover with a lid and let the stock sit for another hour. Strain (reserve the solids if you like to make a second stock), and season to taste with light soy sauce.

3 The broth will keep in an airtight container in the fridge for up to 1 week and in the freezer for up to 4 weeks.

HOW TO COOK RICE

I'm often asked the secret to cooking rice perfectly. There isn't one definitive answer for this as there are a few factors to consider.

First things first: the quality of the rice.

Think about bread and pasta. Generally they only contain a handful of ingredients: flour, water, salt, some have egg, and some have yeast.

But rice? It's just rice and water, so if you want to cook a nice bowl of rice, you've got to start with good-quality rice.

Now we come to the cooking method.

If you are feeling adventurous you could use a stone bowl to cook your rice like the Koreans do, but the easiest way is to use a rice cooker – which, after all, is specifically designed for cooking rice.

Give your rice a good rinse before cooking. Short-grain rice is generally more starchy so you could wash it a few times.

The ratio of water to rice can be affected by the type and brand of rice, but a general rule of thumb is 500 ml (17 fl oz/2 cups) water to 200 g (7 oz/1 cup) rice for long grain, and 375 ml (12½ fl oz/1½ cups) water to 220 g (8 oz/1 cup) rice for short grain.

Of course, some people prefer softer rice and others prefer it to be harder so there is no perfect rule for everyone. All I can say is try, observe, adapt and try again!

FRIED RICE

To many people, fried rice is a creative leftovers dish made with whatever you can find in your fridge, including eggs, spring (green) onions and of course rice. But in fact foodies use this classic rice dish to judge a chef's skill because although it looks very simple, cooking it to perfection requires experience.

Serves 2

2 tablespoons canola oil (or other cooking oil)

2 eggs, lightly beaten

555 g (1 lb 4 oz/3 cups) day-old steamed white rice, chilled

½ teaspoon fine sea salt

1 teaspoon light soy sauce

30 g (1 oz/½ cup) sliced spring (green) onion

1 Heat a large wok over high until the wok is very hot. Turn off the heat, add the oil, then quickly add the egg and cook for about 10 seconds. Turn the heat back on, add the rice and stir-fry to evenly distribute the egg, then lightly press it flat against the wok. Cook for 2 minutes until some of the moisture has evaporated, but the mixture is not too dry. Season with salt, then the soy sauce. Add the spring onion and stir-fry for 10 seconds.

2 Serve immediately.

Optional additions

- meat (chopped ham, Spam or barbecue pork)
- seafood (prawns/shrimp or scallops)
- vegetables (corn, peas, asparagus, mushrooms or Chinese broccoli/gai lan)
- preserved vegetables

Glossary

The following are common ingredients in Hong Kong cooking, which can be found in Asian and Chinese supermarkets or grocers.

CHAR SIU SAUCE
This sweet and spicy sauce is used to lacquer Cantonese barbeque pork, it usually consists of red fermented beancurd, fermented soy bean, garlic, spring (green) onion, soy sauce, sugar, honey and spices. Makes a great marinade.

CHINESE BROWN SUGAR
Made from unrefined cane sugar, Chinese brown sugar is a warm brown colour and sold in small slabs. Not to be confused with palm sugar, which looks similar but is a very different product.

CHINESE CELERY
Similar to celery but with much thinner stalks and a stronger celery flavour. The leaves look very similar to flat-leaf parsley. Goes very well with braised dishes.

CHINKIANG BLACK VINEGAR
Made from fermenting glutinous rice into rice wine, which is then fermented and aged. Black vinegar has a unique fragrance, balance of flavour and hint of sweetness as compared to other vinegars. Chinkiang (Zhenjiang) is the most famous region to produce this type of black vinegar, and only vinegar produced in the region can be labelled as such.

DRIED BLACK FUNGUS
Black fungus is sometimes shaped a bit like an ear, which is why it's also referred to as woodear or cloud ear fungus. It is wavy with a crunchy texture which is great for holding dressings or sauces. It makes an excellent appetiser with sour and spicy dressing and adds texture to steamed dishes where it can soak up juices.

DRIED LIQUORICE ROOT
Looking like dried slices or pieces of wood, dried liquorice root is a popular ingredient in Chinese medicine for its nutritional value. Imparts a distinct liquorice flavour.

DRIED LOTUS LEAF
The huge leaves of the lotus plant, which have a diameter slightly bigger than a basketball. Usually sold dried, the leaves are often used as a wrapper for rice dishes as the rice will take on the delicate fragrance from the leaves when steamed.

DRIED MANDARIN PEEL
Known as *chenpi*, dried mandarin peel is a popular ingredient in Chinese medicine. When used in cooking, it has a unique aroma that goes particularly well with steamed fish. Premium aged mandarin peel can be extremely pricy for its quality (the longer it's aged the higher the price). As compared to the fresh orange mandarin skin, the dried peel is dark brown in colour.

DRIED RED DATES
Chinese red dates are also known as jujube dates. Usually red or dark red in colour, the size varies, but they're usually about size of a thumb (generally the bigger they are, the more premium the quality).

DRIED SCALLOPS
Look for these in your Asian supermarket next to the other dried seafood. They're normally sold in bags and the scallops are about the size of a hazelnut. A specialty Asian dried goods store should have a wider range of sizes to choose from.

DRIED SHRIMP
Available in the dried seafood section in Asian supermarkets, the shrimp are about the size of a peanut.

FERMENTED BEANCURD

Sold in jars, fermented beancurd is firm tofu that has beed inoculated with fungal spores, allowed to dry-ferment, then soaked in brine and usually flavoured with Shaoxing rice wine and chilli.

FERMENTED RED BEANCURD

Similar to fermented beancurd, fermented red beancurd gets its colour from the incorporation of red yeast rice. It has a distinctive flavour and is usually used in braised pork dishes.

JINHUA HAM

A type of dry-cured ham produced in the city of Jinhua in the Zhejiang province of eastern China. Sold in Asian supermarkets alongside the Chinese sausages and other preserved meats. Substitute prosciutto or Iberico ham if unavailable.

KAYA JAM

Kaya jam is a sweet spreadable condiment made from coconut milk and sugar. It's very popular in Singapore and Malaysia and is normally a light yellow–green colour. There is also a caramelised version, which is a darker brown colour.

SALTED BLACK BEANS

Small whole black beans that have fermented with salt, rice wine and *Aspergillus sojae* (the fungus species used to make soy sauce, miso, mirin, etc.). Usually sold in a packet, the beans are quite dry and look a bit like raisins.

SALTED DUCK EGG

Usually available in Asian supermarkets on the shelf alongside the century eggs (the black ones). Salted duck eggs are bigger than chicken eggs and have a richer flavour.

SALTED FISH

The dried seafood section in your Asian supermarket should have a range of salted fish. Look for fish that has been sun-dried for the best quality. Lightly soak the fish in water to rinse off excess salt, steam with a little bit of ginger and eat with rice – simply delicious.

SAND GINGER POWDER

Sand ginger powder is made from dried *Kaempferia galangal*, which is a little closer to galangal than it is to ginger. Confusingly it is, however, sometimes labelled as ginger powder. Ask the staff at your Asian supermarket if they can help you find the right one. You can substitute galangal or ginger powder, but the flavour won't quite be the same.

SESAME PASTE

Toasted white sesame seeds that have been ground to a sauce-like consistency. Usually comes in a glass jar. You can substitute tahini if unavailable.

SESAME POWDER

Ground sesame seeds, usually found next to the whole sesame seeds.

SHAOXING RICE WINE

Shaoxing rice wine is also known as Chinese cooking wine. Fermented from rice, Shaoxing wine, along with soy sauce, is one of the most commonly used ingredients in Chinese cooking. Usually sold in a glass bottle alongside the sauces and vinegars.

SICHUAN CHILLI BEAN PASTE

Chilli bean paste from Sichuan is made from broad (fava) beans (as opposed to soy beans, more commonly used throughout the rest of China). The broad beans are fermented together with fresh local chilli, wine, salt, ginger and sometimes Sichuan peppercorns, to develop the unique flavour that is the soul of Sichuan cooking.

Continued »

SPICY BEAN PASTE

A base of fermented soy bean paste with the addition of stir-fried chilli sauce. Sometimes also contains garlic, ginger and/or shallot. Usually comes in a red plastic or glass jar.

SWEET BEAN PASTE

A base of fermented soy bean paste with the addition of sugar to increase the sweetness. Usually comes in a glass jar or a packet.

WHEAT STARCH

Wheat starch is a fine powdery starch made from wheat that's had the gluten proteins removed. It's a great thickening agent and is used to make *har gow* (shrimp dumpling) wrappers, giving them an almost translucent appearance.

WINTER MELON

A very large type of melon, often double the size of a watermelon. The skin is dark green and the flesh has a very mild flavour, making it a great vessel in broths or soups to soak up the other flavours.

YELLOW GARLIC CHIVES

Similar to the difference between white and green asparagus, yellow garlic chives are garlic chives grown in an environment without much sunlight. Yellow garlic chives have a rounder white stem, are slightly softer and have a milder flavour.

YELLOW ROCK SUGAR

Lumps of crystallised sugar made from unprocessed sugar cane. Most commonly used in dishes like broth or braises to add a hint of sweetness. Usually comes in a box.

About the author

ArChan Chan grew up in Hong Kong during a golden era of growth in the local food scene, eating fish balls and other street food from local hawkers while being exposed to the boom of international influence and the introduction of Michelin-starred restaurants.

ArChan moved to Melbourne, Australia, in 2008 to gain her degree in Culinary Arts at the William Angliss Institute. After working under chef Andrew McConnell for most of her time in Australia (Cutler & Co., Golden Fields and Supernormal), she was head chef on opening Ricky & Pinky at the Builders Arms Hotel, creating a menu of modern Chinese cuisine with a strong influence from her Hong Kong heritage. ArChan now heads the kitchen at LeVeL33 in Singapore.

Index

Published in 2020 by Smith Street Books
Naarm | Melbourne | Australia
smithstreetbooks.com

ISBN: 978-1-925811-62-9

Publisher: Hannah Koelmeyer
Editor: Rachel Carter
Designer: Evi O Studio
Food photographer: Alana Dimou
Stylist: Bridget Wald
Proofreader: Ariana Klepac
Food preparation: ArChan Chan & Meryl Battle

Printed & bound in China by C&C Offset Printing Co., Ltd.

Book 120
10 9 8 7 6 5 4 3 2 1

HONG KONG
LOCAL